PENDULUM
DIVINATION
for Today's Woman

PENDULUM DIVINATION
for Today's Woman

by
Cassandra Eason

foulsham

London•New York•Toronto•Sydney

foulsham

Yeovil Road, Slough, Berkshire SL1 4JH

ISBN 0-572-01975-0

Printed in Great Britain by Cox and Wyman Ltd,
Reading, Berkshire.

Contents

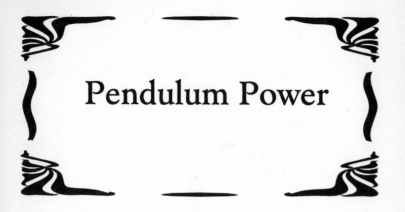

Pendulum Power

The pendulum, a simple weight hanging from a cord, offers one of the most exciting forms of divination. In the hands of experienced diviners it is rated as a far more accurate tool than the traditional hazel twig wand for finding water, oil or minerals.

I have even read about a French naval officer who used the pendulum for seeking enemy mines at sea. But this book is not about finding leaking pipes or blocked drains. For me, the magic of the pendulum lies in the pendulum's power to guide us through the minefield of life.

And for most women, the most pressing question is usually not how to locate running water (in the typical British summer you get far too much of it coming down from the sky), but how to tune in to the flow of life.

What most of us want to know is whether it's

a good idea to quit the job that is about as satisfying as painting the Forth Road Bridge backwards but pays the bills. Or you might be wondering whether you should settle for the guy next door because Mum buys bridal magazines every time you come home and hints you're getting past your sell-by date. On the other hand, perhaps you might decide that marriage to anyone is not for you right now and concentrate on what's bugging Mum so that she needs a white wedding complete with a clutch of Laura Ashley bridesmaids to brighten her existence.

So what exactly is dowsing? 'Dowse' is generally pronounced to rhyme with 'browse' though many Americans rhyme it with 'house'. The word 'dowse' is defined in the Collins dictionary as 'to search for underground water, minerals etc. using a divining rod. This book is mainly about dowsing for less tangible but possibly more vital issues that, if unresolved, can keep us awake at night and distract us from the business of the day.

Women are especially good at dowsing for choices and answers to questions that are vital to their well-being. And the pendulum is a subtle and very portable divining tool. You don't really need a forked hazel twig or metal angle rods when you're trying to work out the state of your love life or finances.

It might create the wrong impression in the bank if you start twitching violently when the bank manager mentions the state of your over-draft.

When I refer to a pendulum I mean any weight on a string or chain, from the inside of a Grandfather clock to a ring, trinket, key or plumb bob from the local DIY shop. Many women choose a quartz crystal pendulum which need not be expensive (more of that in the next chapter) and contains natural earth energies to amplify our own psychic momentum.

There's no doubt as to the validity of dowsing for physical matter whether using pendulum, twigs or metal rods. People all over the world have used dowsing to a high level of accuracy to find wells in areas of drought in the most unlikely places. Indeed, the Swiss pharmaceutical giant Hoffman-La Roche is said to have used dowsers to find water sources for its new sites.

I've included a section on the everyday physical uses of the pendulum later in the book. But you don't need to be an expert in the physical field of dowsing to use a pendulum for focusing your intuitions. Indeed, in spite of grand theories, the physical aspects of dowsing probably tap the same psychic powers, only in a more concrete way.

A pendulum of whatever material is a powerful divinatory aid. You don't need to put your pendulum in a drawer and go back to your Tarot pack or runes (though the pendulum can

Pendulum power

be used with those very effectively) when you need psychic inspiration. Your pendulum can help you to access all the unconscious wisdom buried within you and all the intuitions and inspirations that are bubbling away just under the surface.

Women do find it easier than men to acknowledge their intuitive side and the pendulum is a very flexible way of getting in touch with this inner magic. Emotion plays a vital part in any spontaneous psychic response. The best sort of telepathy occurs when a mum picks up the signal that her child is in danger, whether the child is five or fifty-five years old, and not during card-guessing experiments in a laboratory.

It's the same with dowsing. If an issue matters, whether it's finding water for a drought-ridden town, or deciding whether you should complain because your child's having a hard time at school, then your pendulum will guide you to a successful conclusion.

Dowsing whether physical or mind-delving is then, I believe, primarily need-driven. So you won't find any exercise in this book to practise your skills on finding keys that friends have specially hidden. Any more than I'd suggest that you practise telepathy with your loved ones by guessing what picture they're looking at.

Other people disagree with me on the merits

of practising dowsing and so I've listed socie-
ties at the back of the book you might like to
contact, though they will almost certainly take
a very different approach. I concede that practice at the physical aspects of dowsing may
build up your confidence so that you can
perform publicly without becoming phased. I
know I dowse most successfully physically
when I'm alone with the kids, because they
know all mums are magic and so I don't doubt
my abilities.

On the psychic front, I'm much more confident. Women and not just mums do seems to
have a head start. And for me the pendulum is
primarily of value in the psychic field.

Like many woman, when I need magic, I need
it in a hurry. I don't have the time these days to
wait for a full moon or to slip out at midnight
to hunt for herbs in the woods, like the hedge-
witches of old.

So the pendulum scores because it can be
used psychically for anything, from a 60 second spot check as to whether I should trust a
person I've just met, to a full blown reading on
the merits of trying to steam-roller my eldest
son into a career, or whether to stand back
while he makes a more leisurely entrance to the
world of work and continues to be serviced by
'The Bank of Mum'.

As you will find, there's a direct hot-line via
the pendulum to your psyche using your un-

Pendulum power

conscious muscular reactions (a sort of psychokinesis). It is a method that works best on a personal basis. The responses can be learned in seconds but pendulum readings for other people aren't so effective second hand. Try it.

Time after time, women have used the pendulum to decide between options and almost always they are able to verify the correctness of the choice by the way things turn out in their lives. Perhaps it is easier for women to use their pendulums in this more spiritual area because women automatically use intuition in their daily lives. It's considered OK for men to tramp over wet moors with dowsing rods, but using a pendulum for accessing the inner well of personal wisdom is a different ball game.

However, intuitive dowsing has a long history, although, as you'd expect, the female input is less up-front than the normal, noisy male contrbution.

The method nearest to the way which we are going to make our own magical use of the pendulum, was recorded in the first century AD when Marcellinus, a Roman writer, described a tripod from which hung a ring on a thread. On the circumference of the tripod was a circle showing the letters of the Roman alphabet and the ring swung towards different letters to spell out answers to divinatory questions.

Ignore the predominance in mediaeval woodcuts of earnest broad-hatted gentlemen dowsers that is standard in most works on dowsing. Women are there ,but as usual were far too busy or too wise to stand around while some guy got out his etching pad.

Did you know for example that the word 'dowsing rod' may come from the old Cornish 'dewsys' (Goddess) and 'rhodl' (tree branch)? I prefer this to the more usual Middle English derivation from 'duschen' meaning 'to strike' which comes from early German references to rods striking down towards the ground.

The original master of the divining art was supposed to be the demon Python of the Delphic oracular cult, who could be contacted via a ritual, in which a priestess offered him perfume while holding a rod of wood and reciting magical phrases. The rod holder put her ear to the ground to receive replies that were said to be murmured so low, they could only be heard in the mind.

Dowsing for divination was also practised at Dodona, an ancient sanctuary near Epirus dedicated to Zeus, where priestesses interpreted the sounds of leaves or water under rocks. The rod or magical wand is traditionally female (as you'd expect in its more dubious aspects).

For example, Circe, banished to the Isle of Aenea for poisoning her husband, used her wand to change unwelcome visitors into wild beasts (perhaps it's worth getting your pendulum out when Auntie and the cousins descend

13

on a surprise visit ten minutes before your new man arrives back with the Sunday papers).

And of course there was the ultimate female rod, the broomstick. It was only in the 18th century that broomstick flying was declared legal by Judge Lord Mansfield. But even today, while we can be fairly certain that virgins who step over kitchen brooms won't automatically get pregnant, many a tactless elderly relative refers to a live-in relationship as being 'over the brush'.

My favourite historical female dowser was Lady Milbanke, who so annoyed her son-in-law, the poet Lord Byron, with her hobby (maybe dowsing out his indiscretions) that he wrote after her death: 'She is at last gone to a place where she can no longer dowse'.

I can't guarantee your pendulum dowsing will lead to a sonnet in your honour but you'll find it remarkably easy to learn.

So how does dowsing work? Attempts at scientific explanations have changed over the ages but all seem to stumble on an unknown factor linked with the human psyche. Early explanations talked of signals from the aura of underground water or metal.

Then came ideas of a sympathetic attraction between specific minerals and rods cut from certain trees. Magnetic or electrical influences on dowsers and their rods were the next buzz words, while current theories opt for radiation or waves akin to electromagnetic waves emitted by television or radio stations. But none of these explanations quite fit.

Countless examples of successful dowsing for water or minerals from maps instead of the actual terrain (known as 'remote dowsing') destroy theories of physical forces before we even get on to the less tangible aspects that this book concentrates on. An alternative 'spirit control' explanation has proved just as problematic. As late as 1850, the chemist Chevreul was debating whether, among other factors, a pendulum's movements came from God via the angelic hierarchy or — heaven forbid! — from the Devil and his minions.

Old ideas die hard and recently, when I was giving a demonstration on intuitive rune reading for a large radio station in the south-west, an irate listener rang up to accuse me of summoning up dark spirits in the studio (others complained I wasn't producing rabbits out of hats but that's neither here nor there). You should not have any fears about summoning up occult forces by using your pendulum. The magic is within you and you are not conjuring up demons by asking questions of your pendulum, any more than you are calling up dark powers when the Devil, the card of negative emotions, pops up in your Tarot reading.

This book uses a variation of the *'yes'/'no'* method of questioning the pendulum. Some women find this limiting for more complex issues so I have produced a pendulum cloth (based on the familiar three circle method that you might have met in other books in the *Today's Woman* series). I will also show how you can modify the circles to make instant charts to sort out any problem or to help you to make difficult decisions.

I have also looked at how the pendulum can offer help in diagnosing any weak spots in your health by combining the *'yes'/'no'* method with another easy-to-make 'well-being' cloth. The pendulum involves a very personal, gentle approach and relies on the inner radar we have to alert us when we need either intervention or rest in our health sphere.

A number of people are interested in finding out about their past lives, so I have included a section on using your pendulum for some psychic detective work. Whether we are linking into specific personal past lives, or a more generalised view of a history we shared either personally or though our genetic inheritance, the past can hold the key to many of our present attitudes and reactions.

First we've got to choose our pendulum. This is essentially a personal matter. The finest crystal wand is no more effective than a key on a chain. It is the user who is important. A pendulum is an important statement to the world and to ourselves that we matter and so we should be happy in our choice.

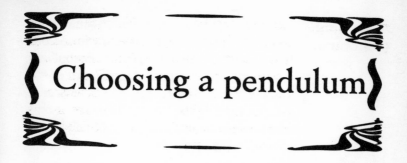

Choosing a pendulum

If you want to start pendulum dowsing right now then you can use the contents of your kitchen drawer. An old key or heavy curtain ring tied to a pencil with a length of cotton wound round it, secured with a paper clip, is perfect. It is not important what you use as the power is coming from within you, it is not in the pendulum itself.

One authority on dowsing, Mr TC Lethbridge, says that you can even use a piece of chewing gum on the end of a thread. The important thing is that you feel at home with what you are using.

The local DIY shop is a good first port of call if you want a very cheap pendulum. A plumb bob on a piece of picture cord is perfect and comes in brass or copper finishes.

However, the most commonly-used pendulums are pointed-ended crystal ones on a single ring and chain. They need not be expensive if you shop around. You may find the lead crystal sort (not natural crystal but beautiful for

Choosing a pendulum

reflecting rainbows) in a local china or gift shop, often hanging in the window for decoration. Quartz crystal ones are sturdier and some women do find the natural energies of crystal a bonus. New Age shops often have a good selection, but go to a shop with clear price tags, lots of choice and plenty of light and handle several pendulums because even apparently identical ones can feel different. Avoid pendulum kits like the plague. Pendulum plus velvet bag plus explanatory leaflet tend to be very expensive.

You may find, as I did, that crystal pendants on ordinary chains are not only cheaper, but also come in a great range of shapes and sizes, so that you are more likely to find something that you feel comfortable with. I got a lovely squat clear quartz crystal, pointed at the bottom and flat at the top held in silver, for under a fiver. Remember, your crystal does not have to fit the traditional pendulum shape.

I slip my crystal through the chain so it's single for dowsing though it's not vital as long as the chain is evenly balanced.

The rest of the time I wear my pendulum as a pendant, so I've always got it to hand for a bit of surreptitious 'mind-dowsing' when needed. It may seem to the outside world as if you're sitting at your desk absent-mindedly swinging your pendant over a memo, whereas in fact, you're using your pendulum for a vital decision. Personal objects such as lucky charms or

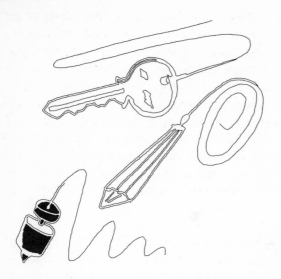

Almost any object can be used as a pendulum

medallions work well, because we endow them with our positive memories and so they are tuned into our emotions. You can use any object that is precious to you, a ring, a childhood lucky charm, a small medallion, your favourite cylinder shaped crystal.

Eventually, you might like to get a more expensive pendulum (perhaps your birthstone). Often women feel guilty about spending money on themselves and yet, even when we are hard-up, we usually manage something for a friend's birthday or a treat for the kids if they are feeling sad. But as your pendulum is something special, cast guilt aside for once and treat yourself.

However, if it's two weeks to pay day and your cash card is sending back 'you must be

Choosing a pendulum

kidding' messages, then the contents of the kitchen drawer really are just as effective and you will find that the key on a piece of string works very well.

If you want a purse or drawstring bag to keep your pendulum so that it won't get scratched, you can usually pick one up quite cheaply at a local fete or market or you can make one very easily. You can then carry your pendulum round in your bag, brief-case or pocket.

The other piece of equipment you will need is an old scarf for drawing circles on (something you may have come across in other *Today's Woman* books). It can be silver, gold, black or white, whatever you like but should not be strongly patterned.

You will also want masses of A4 plain paper, any pen or marker and if you wish a ring binder to keep your divination charts like a diary.

How long should the piece of string, cord or chain on your pendulum be? Some dowsers believe that you have to vary the length of cord according to the object sought and have drawn up complicated (and differing) tables listing the correct length for each metal or element.

That doesn't seem to fit in with the idea that the process operates on a non-material level and experts are constantly arguing about the correct lengths.

Dowsing is a personal art and experiments have shown that if you believe another person's measurements, they will work for you, even in cases when you've misread the charts.

So use whatever length of cord feels right, so that the pendulum doesn't drift aimlessly round (except in a strong breeze) and you feel you can use it on charts without getting a stiff neck. The magic is in you not the technique. I've never come across an agreed measurement for dealing with difficult families.

You can wind a couple of inches round your fingers or, if you use a pencil and cotton, wind up the thread round the pencil until it feels right. I am happy using a chain about eight inches to ten inches long but other people use a longer one.

One of my friends dowses with a cord that's only about five inches long while another practically has to stand on a chair when she's using a pendulum cloth. But both get results that are right for them and that is the real point of the exercise.

There is no point in using someone else's rules if they do not work for you anymore than, if you were a size twelve, you would wear a size eight dress just because it looked good on someone else.

Many people find it most comfortable to hold the pendulum between thumb and forefinger

Choosing a pendulum and wind any extra chain round the forefinger, but that's not a hard and fast rule. Try it out and you'll know what feels right.

It really is your choice. So first get to know your pendulum. Pick a time when you're relaxed, not likely to be disturbed with demands for loo paper from the children, or to be called upon to listen to your flatmate's latest reversal in love. Above all, do it when you're alone.

It's amazing how many of our male partners are 'dowsing experts' after having watched a television documentary on the subject and will make helpful hints on how you're doing it wrong. Or they will set up little tests that you are bound to fail because you're anxious. In the end, you throw the pendulum on the floor and stomp off to sulk or clean up the house, very noisily, at midnight.

But five minutes later there's the old man in front of the mirror, middle-aged paunch and all, asking the pendulum, 'Am I still desirable to women?' and desperately shaking the pendulum to get a positive response. (Fortunately for the male ego, pendulums cannot laugh out loud.)

For today just hold your pendulum and let it swing, no questions, no demands. Feel the link between you. After all it's an expression of your inner world. Then do something nice for yourself because you are pretty special. Sleep with your pendulum under your pillow or

dangling from your bed and enjoy happy dreams.

Day 2

At this stage, all you want to find out is how your pendulum makes its *'yes'* and *'no'* responses and that is very simple. You don't need to ask it questions out loud (a habit that can get you very funny looks).

The 'Yes' and 'No' responses

Whatever you may be told the pendulum isn't an idiot. It's a tangible expression of your psyche. So just let it swing in its own time or give it an initial push if you prefer — like starting cycling downhill to get going.

Eventually the pendulum may circle clockwise or anti-clockwise and whichever seems

**Experiment
with your
pendulum
to find it's
'yes'/'no'
responses**

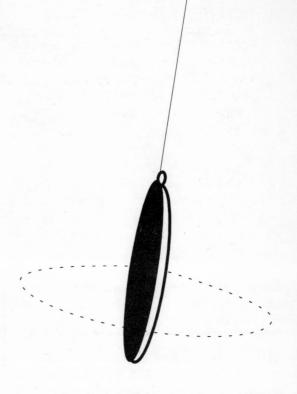

right (or occurs first) is the *'yes'* response. The opposite is often the negative response.

However, for some people the pendulum makes ellipses or a mixture of both ellipse and circle. Listen to your inner-voice and it will tell you which is *'yes'* and which is *'no'*. You don't need to ask your pendulum daft questions like, 'Am I broke?' Later you may find the responses change and become more subtle as your confidence grows (this is useful when you need to dowse unnoticed).

People may tell you that it is just your hand which is moving the pendulum. Of course it's your hand that's moving the pendulum, just as it's your hand that shuffles the Tarot pack or throws the rune stones in other forms of divination. It's why the response is invariably accurate.

Whether we believe we're taking a dip into what Jung called mankind's collective unconscious, or accessing our own inner wisdom and maybe discovering the ability to time-hop, matters less than the fact that the pendulum works. Tell the doubters it's psychokinesis (movement of physical objects by mind-power) and threaten to bend their canteen of cutlery if they don't go away.

Day 3

So you've got *'yes'* and *'no'*. But sometimes we're kidding ourselves and asking the wrong question usually because the real issue is hidden or too painful to look at. For example you might ask, 'Will I be happier if I marry Albert rather than Joe?'

The 'try-again' response

The answer may be 'yes but . . .' or 'no but . . .' If the question is masking a deeper issue — in this case perhaps whether you want to get married to anyone at all right now — your pendulum is very kind and will simply say 'Try again' or 'What's the real question?'. In fact it

The 'try-again' response

acts very much like a sympathetic friend who won't let you con yourself.

The *'try-again'* response for me is the pendulum swinging off at a tangent. However, if your *'yes'* / *'no'* is a circular movement, then the *'try-again'* may be a wild ellipse. Or the pendulum may stop and vibrate mid-swing as if it's staring at you and waiting. And if you ask the real question that's bothering you then you'll get the answer loud and clear — even if it isn't what you expect.

Try feeling the three responses: your pendulum is happy to demonstrate ad infinitum until you feel sure and you don't have to make up appropriate questions. After you're confident with the *'yes'* response do something with the *'yes'* energy, whether making a quick friendly phone call to someone you're miffed with or feel guilty for not contacting or popping some seeds in the garden.

When you're happy with the negative response, get rid of something that's bugging you whether an old grievance or even giving your hidden store of chocolate bars to the kids over the wall.

As for *'try-again'*, maybe a bit of negotiation is called for in a situation you've been adamant about. Or if all's coming up roses you should think about taking up an offer or learn a new skill you thought wasn't for you. The pendulum responses are talking about real issues and the vital part is translating its message into the real world whether it's digging that well or getting out of your chair and grabbing a slice of the action.

A Reading with the Three Responses

I'll show you how someone else used the *'yes'/'no'/'try-again'* response. Anna is in her thirties and had come to a crossroads in her career. I met her on a train journey, we got chatting and she admired my crystal pendant. Before long I'd slipped off my pendulum pendant and Anna was swinging it over her coffee, apparently absentmindedly, as we talked.

A reading for Anna

She had to decide whether to carry on her present, pleasant but undemanding, part-time job at the local Health Centre that fitted in well with her family commitments, or whether to take an update course in her former nursing career and then go on to study for the Health Visiting exams that she abandoned when she became pregnant. Her youngest child had just gone to middle school so the time had come to consider a career move.

> *'Should I take my health visiting exams rather than staying put in my present job?' she asked the pendulum.*

'Rather than' is a quick and effective way of choosing between two options and if you get a straight *'no'* you simply reverse the question. The pendulum twirled round a bit then shot off at a tangent which we decided was Anna's *'try-again'* response. So the question had a complication. When this happens, the best method is to break the question down into very small pieces, tackling each one a step at a time.

I asked her why becoming a health visitor was important, taking the first part of the question first to see if that was the sticking point. If not, I'd have examined the part-time job issue. Her reply was that she'd always wanted to be a health visitor. But people change over time and so do our ambitions. So I suggested that she concentrated on that.

'Is being a health visitor still important to me?' she asked.

The pendulum circled anti-clockwise which was Anna's *'no'*. We'd discovered these responses very quickly while Anna was dangling my pendant idly over her coffee (pendulums aren't sacred and you can easily lend yours to someone you meet as I did to Anna).

So it was possible that Anna's ambitions had changed without her realising over the years. She mentioned that she had seen a social sciences counselling course on offer at the local technical college that interested her but she hadn't seen what use it was towards becoming a health visitor. But now? Anna got off the train saying that she was going to get details of the other course. However, we did not keep in touch and I do not know what happened.

But our brief encounter had at least given Anna a slightly deeper insight into the root of her problems. Armed with that knowledge, she could go on and do something about them instead of wasting time on the wrong course.

The *'yes'/'no'* response can be used to decide pretty important issues but equally well you can use it for a quick decision about something that you are unsure of.

Ask your pendulum a question that concerns you. It does not matter if the issue is life-shattering or mundane, so long as it is an area that is important to you. You can do this in most places, but given that you may get the *'try-again'* response, allow yourself plenty of time and try to be somewhere free from distractions.

If you get the *'try-again'* response then you must try to find what it was about the first question that was the sticking point. In Anna's case it was that although she wanted a career, it was not the one that had been appropriate fifteen years before. Your pendulum might throw up similar changes in your life and it might be a good idea to record the question and answer sessions in your ring binder and date them and keep them in your ring-binder with a date. Then you will be able to chart how and when your aims and ambitions have evolved with the passing of the years.

29

Day 5

Charting your future

Anna's problem was quite straightforward once she'd realised that she didn't want to be a health visitor any more.

But if an issue looks like being very complex involving relationships or strong emotions, you may like to develop a simple flow chart diagram (following the track down through the *'yes'/'no'/'try-again'* responses to work through the options on offer).

Sounds complicated? It's really easy. In its simplest form a flow chart looks something like this.

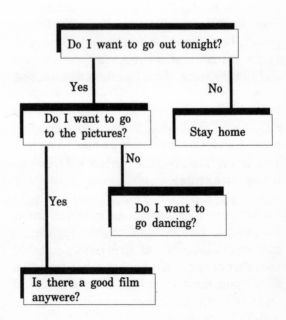

Obviously, for really simple choices you do not need to write anything down or plan out all the different courses of action in detail. But often, when you are confused about some issue then it can help to set things down in black and white. And for the really difficult issues the pendulum can help to clarify things because it can lead you towards choices that you might not have made consciously. Sometimes we need to go against common sense.

You can add an appropriate question at each crossroads. Don't try to plan the chart in advance or you will limit your intuitive thoughts.

Don't think too hard about the initial question either. Write down whatever comes into your head, however unlikely, as this is just a starting place. Remember, if a *'yes'/'no'/'try-again'* issue seems like becoming tangled, you can start a flow chart at any stage in the proceedings.

You may go for weeks without using the pendulum on a major issue, but then you may find that you're consulting it two or three times a week at a crucial time of change.

Even more than the other forms of divination, the pendulum is one that is driven by the need to solve an issue or make a choice. So, unlike the other books in the Today's Woman series which you may have read, I don't suggest you do a daily or even weekly pendulum reading. You will know when it's needed.

This book is divided into days for suggested reading only: don't feel that every time I suggest a new questioning technique, you must carry it out on the day. Do it only if you have something you want to know. Otherwise just read the relevant section and go back to trying the technique when something crops up in the real world.

I suggested that you might like to use a ring binder as a pendulum divination diary as you can then add any charts you make or simply the questions you asked your pendulum. I find it helpful to record readings I do in order to trace how issues change over the weeks.

A reading for Bella

Let me give you an example of a pendulum flow-chart. Bella is in her early twenties and comes from a big united family. She has always spent her holidays at the family cottage in the summer. Her partner, Ian, who doesn't have a family, has been accepted as a full family member and loves the attention. But this year Bella wants to spend the holiday alone with her husband somewhere remote where they can talk, because they've been so busy with their jobs and engulfed by the family, that she feels they've grown apart.

Ian is reluctant to give up the family holiday where he has to do nothing but lie in the sun, be spoiled by the older relatives and go fishing with the lads. Bella realises there's quite a lot at stake and that the holiday is not the real issue but just the focal point. So she chooses a flow chart rather than the basic verbal *'yes'/'no'* method.

A reading for Bella

Bella drew up her first question:

> *Do I want us to have a holiday apart from the family this year?*

The answer, surprisingly, was *'no'* which didn't mean Bella was using her pendulum in the wrong way although she'd expected a *'yes'*. Answers from the unconscious may be totally at odds to our conscious thought but, like most personal divination, can alert us to any unconscious sabotage to our own plans that we are attempting. In this case Bella might have given in 'under pressure' and carried on with the same safe situation only to store up trouble for herself.

The unexpected answer upset all Bella's assumptions and her line of questioning then changed in a way that surprised her as much as the answers.

> *Question 2. Am I using the family to avoid being alone with my partner?*

> *'Yes'*.

> *Question 3. Is there an issue we are avoiding?*

> *'Yes'*.

33

*Question 4. Do I want children in the
near future?*

'No'.

This question was even more of a shock.
'Why did I say that?' Bella asked. But she went
on to explain that Ian was quite keen to have
children as soon as possible, while Mum and
Dad were looking forward to seeing grandchildren romping about on the sands. But secretly
Bella was beginning to feel that was just an
accessory to everyone else's plans.

*Question 5. Does Ian want my family
more than he wants me?*

Try again.

You can't always divine other people's motives, but you can use the pendulum to discover
how you interpret their behaviour deep down
and then check by asking them directly. You
may find your assumptions were wrong.

*Question 6. Am I afraid that Ian wants
my family more than me?*

'Yes'.

Bella needed to talk this one over with Ian.
After a long and very deep discussion, in which
a lot of truths surfaced for the first time, they
eventually decided not only to avoid the family
holiday, but also that Ian should apply for a job

Do I want a holiday apart from the family?

NO

Am I using the family to avoid being alone with my partner?

YES

Are we avoiding an issue?

YES

Do I want children in the near future?

NO

Does Ian want my family more than he wants me?

TRY AGAIN

Am I afraid Ian wants my family more than he wants me?

YES

transfer to the other end of the country, so they could sort themselves out away from the pressures, however kindly meant, of the close-knit wider family unit.

There are no magic answers and the real work has to be done in the everyday world but the pendulum can access the vital clues that can help us to make our own destiny rather than go along with what we allow others to set for us.

Day 6

A flow chart for you

Try setting up a flow chart for yourself using a piece of A4 paper that you can put into your ringbinder. Don't try to map out the questions in advance. Write the first quickly and without too much thought. It may seem irrelevant but can hold the key to the real issue. You may want to hold the pendulum over the question or simply think about it.

Have a *'yes'* side and a *'no'* side of the paper. Put *'try-again'* directly underneath the main question as this is an intermediate stage and then go on to question two.

According to the answer, write down your next question again automatically in the *'yes'* or *'no'* column. You may find that you have nine or ten questions stemming from the first. So make sure you have time to be alone and quiet.

If you want to keep your reading, put a date or number on it so you can look back. As time goes on you will find that you become much more accurate at hitting the vital question first time around. You will also be able to see how far you have managed to stick to your resolutions and how, with the passing of time, the questions change.

At first, most charts look like the path of a sea-sick snail.

Remember, there are no negative responses. Sometimes, if your pendulum answers *'no'*, it does not mean that this is a 'once and forever, set in stone' no. It could mean that, with things as they are just now, that would be the wrong course for you.

And it may be that if you ask the same question if a few weeks or months, the response will have changed. And then you'll see why *'yes'* was not the right answer before.

A Flow Chart Reading for Emma

To illustrate the idea, let's have a look at a flow chart constructed by Emma, a young mother whose five-year-old son, Jim, has been giving her a lot of trouble because of his uncontrollable tantrums.

Although a bright and likeable child, he can cause himself and others a great deal of grief by flying off the handle at the slightest provocation, and sometimes for no reason at all.

Emma feels particularly under pressure as Jim has just started school and there are plenty

A flow chart for Emma of mothers, teachers and helpers who are ready to let her know, in no uncertain terms, that they feel Jim's behaviour is unacceptable (although she has seen other children behaving just as badly but not quite so visibly as Jim).

There is also no shortage of 'experts' on childcare who are ready to offer a great deal of conflicting advice and gloomy diagnoses.

There never is a shortage of experts on such occasions — but sometimes their expertise is open to question.

Emma would like the pendulum to give her detailed advice on how to stop the tantrums. But she knows that, as it is limited to its three basic responses, the best it can do is to help her think the problem through.

So she tackles the problem in stages.

Firstly she divides her piece of paper into a *'yes'* and *'no'* side (*'yes'* on the left and *'no'* on the right). Then she writes down her first question:

Should I change my approach to the problem?

The pendulum's answer is positive. So, working quickly and intuitively, she jots down her questions and answers and produces a chart that looks like this:

Should I change my approach to the problem?

Am I really worried about the problem?

Is the way other people react to Jim's tantrums a problem?

Is it a question of waiting for him to grow out of them?

This put Emma on to a whole new track.

A flow chart
for Emma

Should I offer him incentives to stop the tantrums?

YES

Should I expect a quick solution?

NO

Should I vary the incentives?

YES

Should I ignore the experts?

YES

What has she learned from this session?

Her first question did not really need answering as she obviously does need to change her approach if nothing has worked so far. But your first question is often not so important: it is just a first step to getting somewhere with the pendulum.

Her next two questions are more revealing: Emma would like to think that the problem is not that great and that other people are making too much of it. But the pendulum, with brutal frankness, lets her know that the problem is all too real. It's harsh, but at least it does tell her exactly where she stands.

The pendulum is kinder when she asks it about her reactions to the tantrums. One of the 'experts' was quick to tell her that Jim was only seeking attention and that because she got worked up when he threw a tantrum it made him worse.

She would have liked it if the advice of another self-styled expert' — 'oh he'll grow out of it' — had been correct but the pendulum does not feel that she can play a waiting game.

Other 'experts' have advised stern measures and drastic punishments. But Emma has felt that Jim is the sort of strong-willed child who would die before giving in and that incentives are the correct way to tempt him out of the tantrum phase. The pendulum agrees with her

41

A flow chart for Emma and also tells her to vary the incentives — various little treats such as colouring books, special sweets and TV programmes when he has a tantrum free day (The experts reckoned this was spoiling him). But the pendulum, frank as ever, warned her that even if she took this tack, there was no hope of a quick solution.

As for all the 'experts' . . .

Emma was pleased with this piece of divination as she felt it gave her the information she needed and a path to follow. Above all it gave Emma the answer to the dilemma that had been going round and round her head.

She began varying the incentives and stuck to her guns even through days when it did not seem to be working. But over the weeks her new approach produced the first improvement in ages.

Go over your flow chart if the answer is not obvious. The answer is there and, once you have found it, even if it is not what you really wanted, from then on a situation can only improve. With your own problems you may need more information in which case keep asking the pendulum.

If you feel that a line of questioning is getting nowhere you can always stop, have a cup of coffee or a stiff sherry and start all over again. The pendulum won't get tired.

'Yes'/'no'/'try-again' plus the flow-chart is a very good way of deciding between two options or considering issues that may be interrelated. But sometimes there can be a number of different ways of tackling an issue. Or you may have to choose between several options and then it can get very complicated framing questions to account for all the variables.

The Options Cloth

So for multiple-choice questions you can make a pendulum cloth, based on the three circles with variations format that you may have met in other *Today's Woman* books. All personal divination works on the principle that you've got to decide between options and that the so-called random choice, whether of rune stones, crystals or cards is influenced by the deep intuitive wisdom we all possess.

Once you've learned one *Today's Woman* system the rest can be picked up in no time and before long you'll have a whole battery of methods to choose from according to your mood or need. The only difference with pendulum magic is that we aren't throwing or shuffling anything, but accessing our magical inner knowledge more directly through the pendulum's movements. I find that my pendulum behaves differently when I hold it over a cloth from the normal *'yes'/'no'* responses. But yours may use the normal *yes* response to point out the relevant area. My pendulum vibrates and seems to pull down and I call it the *'this one'* response.

Finding the 'this one' response

But, in either case, some women find that with the cloth it's not an all or nothing reply. They may get the *'yes'* or *'this one'* response over one section and maybe a weaker *'yes'* or *'this one'* over a second section, if the question needs two joint methods of resolution.

First establish your own *'this one'* response. You don't need to set up one of those amazing tests which are sometimes suggested: like having a pile of cream buns, a plate of lettuce and a dish of nutritionally balanced reconstituted splodge and asking the pendulum which one is best for you. Ten to one the pendulum will drag you over to the cream buns with a big grin. It's not the pendulum who's the idiot!

Simply think about observing a *'this one'* response. You can do this even before you make the cloth. Wait and you'll feel the pull and vibration or if you get the *'yes'* response as usual then that is fine.

Now try out your new response in real life. Go to a garden centre, wait till no-one's around and hold your pendulum over three pots of herbs or flowers without reading the labels. Buy the one that your pendulum chooses. Then take it home and offer the pendulum the choice of three or more bits of garden or, if you haven't got a garden, ledges in the house or window-box.

Plant your herbs or plants in that spot and offer a bit of tender, loving care. Real emo-

44

tional decisions can't be created for test purposes but it's nice to establish confidence in your response. The pendulum does not have to involve tests of skill, psychic or otherwise and you've got nobody to please with the results but yourself. As the herbs or plants grow, you will have a reminder that it's making the choice and carrying it through that matters.

Whether you end up taking first prize at Chelsea Flower Show or with only enough parsley to decorate the smallest sandwich, at least you have made a start. It's not 100 per cent or your money back in life. No fortune teller's predictions however expensively bought can guarantee everlasting happiness or instant success.

At the worst you will end up with something green in a bare place. But, who knows? Next year you might have a whole forest.

Day 8

To make the cloth, you can use an old scarf or piece of cloth a foot to eighteen inches square on which you will draw your three circles.

The Circle of Self
With an indelible marker (use any colour that shows up well on the type of cloth you have chosen) draw round a saucer or use a compass to make a circle about that size. You can draw free-hand if you wish. This circle represents the *inner world of the essential, real you* that

Making the Options Cloth.

45

The three circles

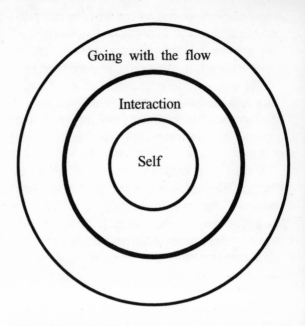

Going with the flow

Interaction

Self

was you when you were five and will be there when you are ninety five.

If your pendulum homes in here, then you will know that the way forward is by establishing your priorities and going it alone with no free rides or soft options. Any change you may have to undergo may not even be a physical one, more an awareness of your own unique identity and separateness even from those you love most.

Right now it's your own happiness and not the happiness of others that is important. Many women find this idea difficult to cope with and fear they are being selfish and worse still that they'll be lonely. But we can feel isolated in the middle of a crowd and if you don't love yourself you can't make others happy.

At first some women, especially wives or mothers, find it hard to let the pendulum pull them here, but it's where your inner voice lives so it may be important to listen. Because right now the advice of others is misleading and where vital principles or issues are at stake you can't in this instance ignore your own certainties.

Move your pendulum over this circle and feel the boundaries that mark out where you end and others begin.

If you happen to be in the middle of the best ever love affair, you'll find this irrelevant. But no matter how much we love someone else, we have to hold on to our identity if the love is to survive after the initial intensity.

So do something now, however small, that would make you happy — it doesn't have to involve money — whether cooking something you like, taking half an hour out for a bath, a read, a walk or simply writing a list of all your achievements and strengths.

We've all got strengths of some sort and you may be surprised when you tot yours up to find what a great person you are and decide at least for a while not to let anyone put you down or short-change you.

Day 9

Interaction

The Circle of Interaction

Draw the middle circle round a tea plate (you'll get just as good results from jumble sale crockery as Crown Derby). Or use a compass to get a circle about this size.

This circle represents the area where you have to meet the outside world half-way, the circle of *negotiation and compromise.* Sometimes it's hard to listen to what the other person is really saying and not to what you imagine they will say.

We often shoot ourselves in the foot before we start because we're listening to yesterday's news. So when the pendulum directs you to this circle, it's not a time to sit on your high horse or go off in a huff. If the other guy's getting het up, it may be that he's replaying yesterday's rejections and you need to spell out what you mean and don't assume that he understood first time.

Or you may find that your ambitions and dreams have to take account of the needs of those around, whether it's a temporary situation, a sick relative, or a friend that needs emotional support, or the ongoing commitments to family or partner.

For many people, the solitary journey to the fast track doesn't mean happiness and a balanced and fulfilled life can integrate both our caring and competitive qualities. But that can mean compromise and a constant juggling act and this is where the middle circle is vital in keeping the balance.

To apply this to your real world, pinpoint an area where you are blocked from fulfilling a plan or goal, whether something small like a day away from the kids or time to follow an interest. See if you can find a way round any obstacles by enlisting the help of a sympathetic colleague, friend or family member, or perhaps by a bit of bartering of favours. Usually there are ways round obstacles if we persist and are prepared to compromise.

The Circle of Going with the Flow

Draw round a dinner plate or use a compass to make the third outside circle. This circle talks of living for now on other people's terms and not standing out for your rights or going it alone.

Going with the flow

There are times when it's best to go along with the way life is and not as we would like it to be. We can all waste time and energy regretting the opportunities we never took, the places we never visited and the perfect guy we didn't meet, instead of making the most of the life we are living, warts and all.

Nothing's perfect and maybe, if you look on the bright side, you'll find it's better than you think.

Even if you are in a situation where you feel

alienated or misunderstood, go along with it
for now while preparing the ground for improvement or change. If you tell the boss to get
lost, you may not get another job in time to keep
up the mortgage payments. So until you are
ready to leave you will have to grin and bear it
and use what might seem like negative, wasted
time, whether in the world of work or relationships, in a positive way.

Unlike the middle circle, you're not going to
get far by negotiation. But that's not all bad
because sometimes by sticking with a situation
or relationship that seems boring or unsatisfac-
tory you come out into the sunshine and find
you're glad you didn't give up. And you may
find that you've learned a great deal from the
other person/people when the pendulum moves
again to the centre or second circle.

When you hold your pendulum over this area,
try to find something positive about every day.
Counter any negative aspects in your day by
contacting people who make you feel good and
avoid those who you know will only moan.

Of course, you may say that everything's fine,
in which case you won't need the last circle
right now and maybe won't ever need it. As I
said the pendulum is for you to use as and when
you need it and most of us don't need a
pendulum to tell us if we're happy — certainly
not unless we're prepared to have the pendulum alert us that maybe we're kidding ourselves a bit in some area.

Divination is like a psychic traffic sign system. It can tell you that there's a sharp corner ahead but it does not say that you are definitely going to crash on it.

A Reading for Rowan Using the Three Circles

Rowan is a lone mother of a teenage son and has a well-paid job as an administrator. Her new boss is making her life a misery because he objects to working mothers. She gets on well with colleagues, however, and thanks to the new boss, there are training schemes that can be fitted in with office hours. But she feels she's had enough of his constant sniping and back-biting and that the job is not worth the aggravation.

The pendulum swung around and then homed in on the Outside circle of Going with the Flow. So for now the pendulum seems to be advising her to stick at the situation. In twelve months time, her son will have left school and things will be easier financially and she can look for a job where the money is perhaps less but the job satisfaction is greater. On the other hand, in twelve months time Rowan will have completed the firm's computer course and so may be qualified for even better alternative employment or promotion to another branch of her present firm.

For now there's no point in wasting energy on what she can't change though there is no inbuilt

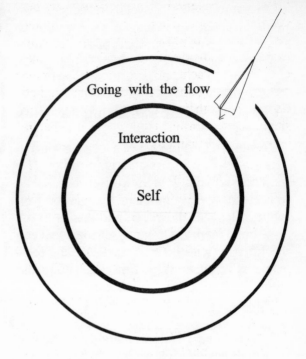

Going with the flow

Interaction

Self

clause about being a doormat to her boss.

Maybe for now she should concentrate in enjoying the company of her colleagues at work and, now her son is older, building herself a social life of his own. Rowan too can begin to develop new friendships outside work to offset the negative aspects of her life.

Rowan was a bit disappointed. 'But I knew that already,' she said. 'I wanted to be told if I walked out I'd get a brilliant new job. Or the boss would realise the error of his ways and increase my salary, or leave, or suddenly become sweetness and light.' I asked her why she had left off her psychic shopping list the unattached guy with pots of money who would take her off on his yacht and feed her grapes for the rest of her long and happy life? She laughed because we both knew that however much you shell out for a fortune teller you can't change reality into fairyland by magic.

One of the strengths of the pendulum is that it does tell you what you already know deep down, but maybe don't want to acknowledge. And if that means sticking out a no-win situation for a while but extracting every benefit from it while waiting for the right time for change, then at least you're not fretting or sitting in your ivory tower expecting rescue.

Now try a three circle reading for yourself, using your cloth if there is an issue that concerns you or you've a decision to make. Decide on the issue. If you're not clear, use your *'yes'/ 'no'* to ask if this is the real issue and move your pendulum slowly over the circles, several times if necessary, till you feel a pull, vibration or *'yes'* response.

You will then know if it's best to go it alone or to concentrate on your own happiness and future. Or does happiness right now lie in the middle circle, in compromise and finding ways of fulfilling your personal dreams, albeit modified, while meeting the needs of those close to you? On the other hand should you, like Rowan,

Day 12

The Outer Areas

go with the flow of the outer circle and accept that the present situation means that you need to accept a less than ideal situation and look for happiness in other areas of your life?

The Outer Areas of the Cloth

Often a three-circle reading is enough to clarify your ideas. But you may feel that while it's useful to determine whether to stick out for what you want, compromise, or go with the flow. You may need to know more, for example, how do you react in everyday life to your grotty teenager, stroppy boss or free-wheeling partner or even the feeling that you want to add excitement to your life? If the choice is between jetting off to Barbados with a new lover or staying home to fix the oil leak on your car you're hardly going to need a pendulum to help make the decision.

The four outer quadrants of the cloth beyond the circles can be used after a circle reading to identify the most appropriate course of action. You'll simply divide this area into four using the quarter of an hour positions on a clock. Each segment represents one of what the ancients believed were the four elements: *Earth, Air, Fire* and *Water*.

From early times these elements have been linked with human qualities. More recently, Jung theorised that each related to a particular way that the mind functions. In the system that we will adopt, *Earth* deals with a practical approach and using your common sense; *Air* speaks of a logical but determined approach; *Fire* requires you to reshuffle the pieces of a problem to come up with an off-the-top of your head solution and *Water* suggests taking an empathic, intuitive response to a person or situation.

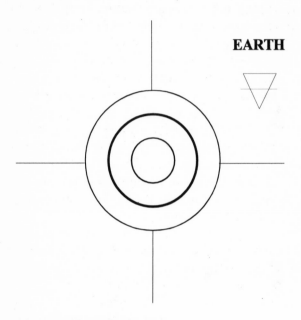

EARTH

The Earth Quadrant

The top or northern quadrant will be *Earth*. It runs from the 12 to 3 o'clock position on the cloth. Draw the horizontal lines for the quadrants outside the three circles. You can draw the symbol for this as the old alchemical sign of an inverted triangle with a horizontal line through it. You can colour it green if you want to. It will look nicer, but it will not function any better because, as I always stress, the magic is within, you not in the cloth nor the pendulum.

Earth represents the practical approach, whether drawing up rotas to make organisation of your daily work or home life more efficient and less of a burden for you, withdrawing practical help if you are doing more than your share, or if a cause is worthwhile by rolling up your sleeves.

When you are pulled to this quadrant you must adopt the step-by-step strategy of the legendary tortoise that is left behind by the hare, but plods on, never giving up, and invariably gets there before the fast-track merchants.

The pendulum only confirms what you already know: that there may be a bit of slog involved in whatever area you want to develop or even in your life generally, but that your ideas are practical and rooted in good sense and firm foundations. So it's a very positive area of the cloth.

It can be very satisfying after you've drawn this quadrant to make a small practical change to improve your life. Perhaps touching up some scruffy paintwork or reclaiming a small patch of garden that is unloved.

Or on your next free day you could take a trip, either alone or with someone who makes you feel happy but doesn't demand constant chatter. Go into the country or visit an ancient stone monument where you can feel close to the earth and part of the slow continuing tradition. Perhaps on your travels you'll find a piece of crystal. Sometimes holding the most ordinary looking pebble to the sun will reveal its transparency. Whatever you find take it home as a sign that life can't always be hurried.

The Air Quadrant

The second quadrant, to the right and east, will be *Air*. This is marked between the 3 and 6 o'clock positions. The alchemical *Air* sign is an upright triangle with a line going horizontally through it. You can colour this yellow if you wish.

Air uses thought and logic rather than emotion. But once you have decided on that course of action, *Air* insists that you go straight for it and that your ambition does not end up as a load of empty angry words or hot air.

When your pendulum is drawn towards the *Air* quadrant, it's a signal for you to move back from an issue or decision (especially if it is one that involves a lot of emotion) and weigh up the pros and cons in a detached way as though you were advising someone else. You could even write the for and against points and dowse over them.

When you've drawn your *Air* quadrant, you might like to spend some time doing a crossword puzzle or a jigsaw, or even reading the

The Air Quadrant

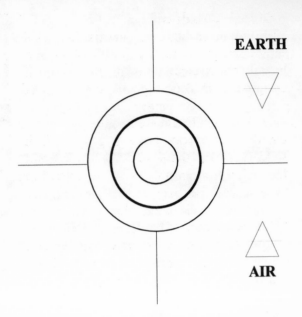

EARTH

AIR

manual for your word processor (after all, you can't keep blaming the machine for things that don't work).

Or you could take the bull by the horns and do half an hour's essential paperwork whether tax, accounts or filing all your insurance documents and receipts.

On your next day off, perhaps you could climb to the top of a hill, however urbanised it is, and feel the wind on your face and watch the clouds moving, uncluttered by the trivia that can clog our energies. You could even try flying a kite just to get the feel of riding the air.

The Fire Quadrant

The bottom or southern quadrant is *Fire*. This runs from the 6 to the 9 o'clock position beyond the circles and its sign is simply an upright triangle. You might like to colour it red.

Fire tells you to use the solution that comes unbidden into your head. It represents the sudden change, the snap decision, or simply the resolve not to be pressurised into answering right now if none the options feel right.

The Fire
Quadrant

If the pendulum pulls towards the *Fire* quadrant and an instant, if unexpected, answer doesn't spring to mind, then move back from

EARTH

FIRE

AIR

the issue if only for a short while. Rearrange the pieces, look at the issue from a new angle and try a third solution usually one you rejected as impractical, or risky which ultimately may prove the best.

When you have drawn the *Fire* quadrant, try to do something that gives you pleasure or is creative. This does not have to be a painting in the style of Picasso or eighty thousand word novel. Surprise others with an impromptu and instant party, whether spaghetti and music with flatmates or a McDonald's with the kids.

On your next day off, if it's sunny, go out and feel the warmth. If it's mid-winter it's a good excuse to light a real fire and interpret the pictures formed by the flames. You can do this with candlelight if your house has all-electric underfloor central heating.

Day
15

The Water Quadrant

The left or western quadrant is *Water*. This runs from the 9 to the 12 o' clock position. Its sign is an inverted triangle and can be coloured blue.

The Water
Quadrant

Water tells you that all may not be as it seems. So dig below the surface to try to understand the underlying motives, fears and feelings of others. Above all, listen to your own gut feelings and intuitions as to whether a person or situation is to be trusted. Let yourself go with the flow for now and see what happens.

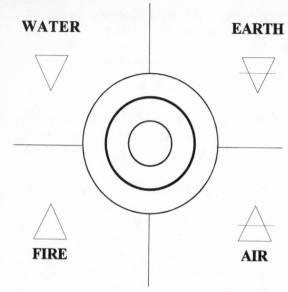

WATER   EARTH

FIRE   AIR

If the pendulum draws you to this quadrant, then it may be that you are feeling out of touch with yourself and others and so missing the vital signals that normally guide you as to the best action.

Re-read a favourite book, watch an old weepie on video, or take a deep soothing bath with fragrant blue or green salts.

On your next day off, try to find a river, lake, the sea, or even the local duck-pond and sit by it for a while. Or have a deep long fragrant bath. Or even go to the local swimming pool — you don't have to be an Olympic standard swimmer to lie back and let the water support you and paddle with the flow. If you are very

Day
16

resourceful you might combine all four elements in one day.

There are two ways you can use your outer quadrants. You can do a circle reading first and then pass your pendulum over the outer quadrants and see which element or elements the pendulum draws you to.

Alternatives for the outer quadrant

Or you might like to use the outer quadrants entirely separately maybe after a simple *'yes'/ 'no'* session with the pendulum or independently. If you've got a day when you know you'll have decisions to make or is an important one, you might even like to use this method first thing in the morning to give you a quick guide as to the best approach.

Claire used only an outer quadrant reading because she knew what she wanted to do. The only problem was which tack to take to achieve her goal while causing the least hurt to others involved.

A Reading for Claire

She is approaching retirement and her children are delighted because then Mum will suddenly become available for looking after grandchildren during the day. Her eldest daughter is already planning a full-time return to work on the strength of it.

But no one has asked Claire if she wants to settle down to being full time gran. Indeed, she only discovered the role which had been planned for her when one of her grandchildren mentioned what fun it would be spending every day at Gran's house.

But Claire has other plans. She has worked full-time since her husband walked out twenty years before, leaving her with two small children. Claire viewed retirement as a time to up sticks and move to Normandy, which she has always loved and use her fluent French to join in with local activities. On the other hand she doesn't want to hurt the family.

Claire passes the pendulum over the four outer segments and it swoops down over *Earth,* the practical solution. What can it mean? Take up knitting so she can snooze in her chair while her grandchildren play merrily at her feet?

No. It's saying that it's time for her to take practical steps to follow her dream, if that is what she really wants, so it will be all cut and dried and too late to change by the time daughter gets round to officially breaking the news to mum of her new post as Mary Poppins.

She decides to put her house on the market and take a long break to Normandy to look for suitable properties, remembering that she will need an extra bedroom for visitors. And for starters she is going to teach her grandchildren French, so they can fit in when they visit.

Now try a reading using the four outer seg-

A reading for Claire

ments only. You don't need to spell out if it's a love, money, family or career issue. You will find that the suggested strategy might apply to your life generally or to a particular issue, in which case it will be crystal clear.

Try a morning reading to determine the best strategy for the day. Hold the pendulum a few inches above the cloth, you will know the right distance and move from segment to segment until you get your this one response.

The pendulum methods can be combined as you wish at different times, although you may prefer to stick to just one or two favourite ways. All that you have to remember are your *'yes'/ 'no'/'try-again'* and maybe *'this one'* responses. It really is as simple as that.

Day 17

A reading with the whole cloth

Try this for a really complex or important issue. You may find it helpful to keep recordings of your readings — a quick sketch on a piece of paper, dated and put in your ring binder, is a good reminder as the months go by of how far you have travelled and how, sometimes, a seemingly life and death issue turned out not to matter that much after all — usually because something else has taken its place.

A Reading for Kerry

To see how it works, let's eavesdrop on a reading of a woman who used the whole cloth to decide what was for her a vital issue. Kerry is sixteen and her parents have split up. She adores her dad but hates the young woman he has moved in with. Her mum with whom Kerry lives is very depressed and won't let Kerry talk about her Dad.

Kerry hasn't done well in her GCSEs, which is hardly surprising considering all the tension at home. But she doesn't want to re-take them. Dad suggests that she lives with him and pregnant girlfriend when they move to the other end of the country in the near future and that Kerry helps with the baby in return for her keep.

Mum, on the other hand, is putting pressure on Kerry to go back to school and says that if she moves out, she needn't bother to keep in touch. Kerry loves horses and has been offered a job living in at some stables a few miles away where she has riding lessons, plus a day a week release for college. But both Mum and Dad oppose that proposal and say that if she blows it, then she needn't come running back to them for help.

Poor old Kerry! No wonder she prefers horses! First she holds her pendulum over the circles and, unerringly, the pendulum homes for the *innermost circle of self*. It seems to be indicating that she should go it alone — a big step when you are only sixteen and the grown-ups in you life are behaving like children.

But at this time the other options for Kerry are the devil or the deep blue sea: looking after the

A circle reading for Kerry

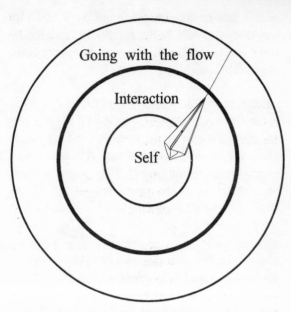

Going with the flow

Interaction

Self

baby of a woman she dislikes while Dad tries to keep everyone happy; or back to school while living with Mum, which Kerry doesn't want to do either. What she has always wanted is to work with horses.

So really there's not a lot for room for negotiation and Kerry can't go along with both parties' wishes. She is left with the stable job which gets her away from the battlefield and gives her a roof over her head and training in an area that she enjoys. This is not an ideal solution but it will give the so-called adults time to sort themselves out and realise, perhaps, how unfair they are being.

Unfortunately, as I have said before, there

aren't any magical solutions. But if you find yourself trapped between the devil and the deep blue sea, even a leaking life raft is better than nothing.

But how should Kerry proceed with the minimum of hassle, accepting that a fair amount of hassle is inbuilt in the situation? Kerry next tried the outer segments and the pendulum went for the *Air* option, which suggests that she should ignore all the emotional pressures and think logically about what is really best for her.

Then it will be a question of going for what she needs and ignoring everybody else's aggravation, which may turn out to be nothing more than hot air when they see how determined she is to live her own life and not tidy up after their mistakes.

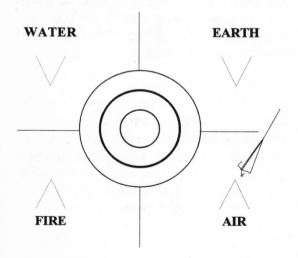

WATER

EARTH

FIRE

AIR

A circle reading for yourself

Now try a full cloth reading for yourself. You can do it now or wait until you feel the time would be right.

Usually we all have some vital question in our lives however happy we may be — perhaps tossing up whether to marry the prince, the millionaire or sign a multi-million pound film contract and live in solitary splendour (well I can dream!)

But if you don't feel it's the right time to do a full reading, then wait. The great Pendulum Mistress in the sky isn't holding a stop-watch and counting off the seconds until you swing your pendulum.

When you feel ready to go ahead, concentrate on the issue while holding the pendulum slowly over each of the circles. See which one it pulls towards, vibrates over or gives a strong *'yes'* response to — whichever is your *'this one'* mode.

Then try the outer segments. If the pendulum seems to pull towards two at the same time or hover between them, it does not mean that you are doing something wrong but that there is not a clear-cut solution to the problem and you need to resolve it with a combination of two approaches: ie logic followed by practical action may be the way forward.

Don't forget to record your results if you are keeping a pendulum folder.

If you want to focus on a specific issue or area of concern then you may, on occasions, want to make a quick personalised pendulum chart rather than using the general pendulum cloth. You can prepare a set of blank three-circle pages in your folder, or draw them at the time you need one on any spare paper to hand.

Day 18

You can even scribble circles on the backs of envelopes, old memos, or the kids' jumble sale letters, while at work or on the train. Your pendulum will oblige by discriminating between quite small areas. I've even got a couple of circles that I have drawn at the back of my diary. You can subdivide the circles to include as many options as you wish. Use the quadrants round the circles as well either like the ones on the pendulum cloth for *Earth, Air, Fire* and *Water* or as extra option areas.

Making an options chart

As I have said, there is no Pendulum Mistress checking you're abiding by the rules. These rules are only made up by people who find a method useful, but over time the rules tend to get enshrined as holy writ. I've had people on radio phone-ins getting very heated because their book of divination insists that you must follow certain steps in a certain order or else! But at the end of the day, magic really is a personal issue and we can get so lost in ritual we lose sight of the purpose.

But I would advise you very firmly that if you're on a busy commuter line or in a crowded wine bar, you need to watch how you label your circles, especially if you're dowsing on the subject of your exotic love life, or are planning a massive fraud. You don't want nosey parkers staring over your shoulder and running off to tell the tabloids or the Boys in Blue. I'll use the next couple of days to give you a few examples I've come across as these personalised pendulum charts are such a useful and accurate method, though on most occasions when I've time and privacy I use my pendulum cloth.

Day 19

A financial chart

Few of us need the pendulum's advice on spending money. The problems usually come at an earlier stage: finding the resources for a special holiday, an extension on the house, a newer car or a very hungry overdraft. Think of the pendulum as your inner bank manager who says 'how' rather than 'no'.

The inner circle might perhaps be labelled 'finding a cheaper way to attain your goal'. The middle circle might be 'taking out a loan' (offers pour through the door with every post but, as I tend to forget, they have to be paid back). The outer circle could represent saving the money by doing overtime or getting an extra job.

A Reading for Sarah Jane

Let me tell you about Sarah-Jane who drew up a personal financial chart. She had just left school and was planning a holiday job before college to earn enough to visit her sister who is

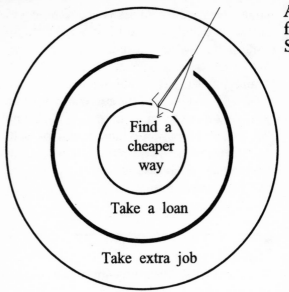

Find a
cheaper
way

Take a loan

Take extra job

A reading
for
Sarah-Jane

living in the United States. But the job as a temporary nanny in London had fallen through and alternative employment was hard to find. How could she raise the cash? She used the three basic circles without the outer quadrants.

The pendulum veered straight towards the inner circle (finding a cheaper way). This was much as she had expected but even so, it's worth going over all the circles even if you get a response in the first you come across.

And that was Sarah-Jane's answer. The question of not going didn't even enter into it. The outlay for the fare was the stumbling block, so

Sarah-Jane made inquiries to see if there was any way she could get her fare paid in return for work in the United States.

Nannying was out because of visa problems but she discovered that she could get a job as a Camp Counselor in with the U.S. Camp America organisation which would pay her fare and allow her two free weeks to travel. It worked out well and Sarah-Jane is going back next year in her summer vacation to visit a guy she met on the plane.

Day 20

Flow charts and circles

A Reading for Tim

When you are dealing with a particularly tricky problem then you might find it helpful to combine the circles with a flow chart. In this case the pendulum was used by a rather sceptical man. Tim was nagged into action by his wife Sue. Of course, he didn't believe a word of it before or after, although Sue says that she has since seen him using the plumb bob from his tool kit, for other purposes than making sure that shelves are hung correctly.

Tim and Sue bought a house in the Wiltshire countryside in just the area they wanted to live in and bring up children. But although Tim had hoped to do a lot of his business from home this did not work out and he found himself spending more time in London.

He had a room in a friend's house. But this was not really very convenient as Sue did not get on with these particular friends all that well and she and the children could not visit him there.

A reading for Tim

One day, Tim's work took him to Little Venice where the canal runs through Westminster and he saw a canal boat for sale and fell in love with the idea of living on the water. He reasoned that if he had his own base in London Sue and the kids could visit when they wished. The boat was small but affordable — just — and Sue, who had had a number of very happy canal holidays in her teens, was very keen on the idea. But on his next weekend at home Tim seemed to go cool on the idea.

He couldn't give any definite reasons for this cooling-off and put it down to a gut feeling. This seemed a rare case of male intuition so Sue decided to put it to work and gave him her pendulum. She tried to teach him how to use it but, like most men, he knew best and used a system which worked for him. Sue, when she tried it later, was surprised to find it worked for her as well which only goes to show that when it comes to rules for the pendulum, the only ones that work are the ones that work for you.

Tim started off with a flow chart but divided his sheet of paper into three sections: *'yes'* on the left, *'no'* on the right and *'try-again'* in the middle. He didn't hang around to get to know Sue's pendulum and its *'yes'* and *'no'* responses, but instead dowsed on the sheet of paper with it, letting it draw him towards the

A reading for Tim

'yes', 'no' and *'try-again'* sections.

His flow chart looked like this after his first question, 'Do I want the boat?' got a *'try-again'* response from the pendulum.

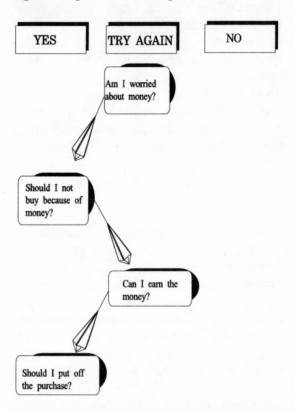

| YES | TRY AGAIN | NO |

Am I worried about money?

Should I not buy because of money?

Can I earn the money?

Should I put off the purchase?

His last question swung him into the 'NO' area.

The pendulum had asked Tim to think again about his first question because it was not the real issue. He certainly wanted the boat, as did

Sue and the kids, who were looking forward to canal holidays on Daddy's Floating Bedsit.

Tim's real worry — and one that he would not admit to himself — was financial. Some people, if they really want something they know they cannot quite afford, will dash out and buy it and worry about the consequences afterwards.

Tim was the type of person who will deny themselves something that they think they cannot afford and then mope about it. They do not tell anyone the real reason for their sulks and instead keep saying: 'Oh I don't really want that after all.' But all the time, deep inside, they are aching for it.

The pendulum at least brought the money fear out into the open. Tim's inner voice was telling him that he could earn the extra money to pay for the boat if he really wanted it badly enough.

So far, so good. But this session was a little bit inconclusive. So Sue suggested that he try the circle method.

Quickly, she drew three circles by hand, not bothering to get them exactly right, and wrote in them the three courses of action which were open to Tim.

In the centre she put 'Do Without', in the inner circle 'Earn More' and in the outer circle 'Loan'. The circles then looked like this:

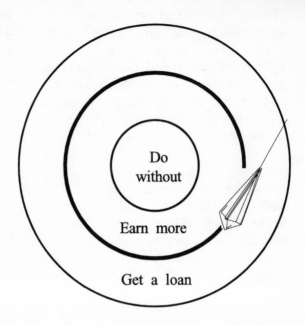

Do
without

Earn more

Get a loan

Tim was persuaded to hold the pendulum over the three circles and, not surprisingly, found the pendulum swaying between 'Earn more' and 'Loan'. So they went ahead with the purchase, managing to find a marine mortgage company which gave them an 80 per cent loan.

Tim also realised that having a base of his own in London meant that he could do a little extra freelance work in the evenings, because he did not have to fit in with anybody else's hours and could burn the midnight oil if he needed to.

Sue managed to make a few economies and, as far as I know, the boat plan is working very well for them.

You can also draw up a chart for plotting your way forward in life. The Inner Circle might represent going flat out for your dream. The middle circle could involve combining achieving a future ambition more slowly to fit in with your present lifestyle. And the outer circle could be enlisting the help of others to set you on your path.

A Reading for Vicky

Vicky's chart was even more specific in its labels, although she used only the three circle format. Vicky wanted to be a novelist but found it hard to combine writing with her full-time job as a teacher. Since her children were adults, money wasn't so short.

Charting your ambitions

But her partner felt that she should keep her writing as a hobby for evenings and the holidays until she actually sold something. Vicky labelled her inside circle 'giving up work for a year, writing full-time and then sending her work to every publisher in the land'. You can label the circles as fully as you like or just use a single word. the important thing is that you are clear in your own mind about what they represent.

The middle circle involved cutting down her teaching hours to make time for writing in the day and taking a writing course to improve her skills. The third circle was the line of least resistance, going along with her husband's wishes and sending samples of her work to an agent to see if she had any talent or should keep

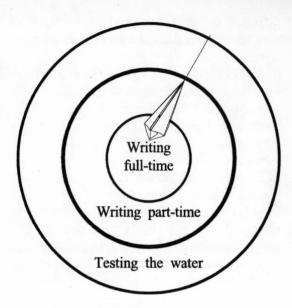

Writing
full-time

Writing part-time

Testing the water

her writing as an hobby.

Vicky's pendulum went to the inside circle and ignored all the others. In fact the way Vicky had labelled her circles meant it was an either/or choice. This surprised me as Vicky seemed a very gentle, compliant person. But Vicky said it confirmed what she hadn't put into words but felt inside. All her life she'd gone along with what other people wanted and needed and now she was determined to have one year fulfilling her dream that had waited on the sidelines.

She'd supported her husband for several years financially while he was building up a business and now she felt it was her turn. The pendulum confirmed her inner conviction and she was happy that if after a year she wasn't getting anywhere she'd accept her dream was just a dream.

But that's not real magic, you might say. The pendulum didn't tell her she was going to be a bestseller.

No, it didn't. Nor did she even bother to ask that because she knew it was the wrong question. To get even to the door of the best-seller stakes takes a lot of very hard slog (plus good luck, but even that depends on your having a saleable product). Vicky knew that but it did not worry her. She also knew that by far the majority of writers go along selling a few thousand books here, a few thousand there but getting great satisfaction from being published.

The pendulum isn't the type of magic wand that can kit you out with a pretty frock. Nor can it turn mice lurking in the understairs cupboard into coachmen and a cabbage into a golden coach. Nor, for that matter, can it turn your old man into Prince Charming.

But the pendulum can confirm your deep-down conviction that now is the time to go for that dream. Even if you don't make it at least you had the fun of swimming in the water, not standing on the edge of life wishing you'd got the courage to dip your toe in. And going for it and, perhaps, getting a short story published or even a full-blown book, that's real magic. The most expensive clairvoyant in the world can't

A reading for Vicky

guarantee you a lifetime of love and happiness and not a drop of rain except at night to water the roses. So you might as well use your money for making life better right now. I argue this time and time again when I'm talking to people.

I could be very rich if I predicted golden futures all round and moved my pitch on when people realised it wasn't going to happen (and some folks will wait many, many years). The magic is in the way the pendulum moves, or the cards, runes or crystals fall, to pinpoint what, deep inside, was waiting to come out. It might even be even the stirrings of change that will soon loom large on your horizon.

What if you get the *'try-again'* response for all your circles or no reaction at all? In that case it may be that what you're asking isn't realistic or the real crux of the issue. Will I become a best-seller? is not a question that the pendulum is qualified to answer. If you really want to write, you will write. So try to find the issues that are really at the heart of the matter. You can always use your simple *'yes'/'no'* response if it's a sticking point, to get things moving.

If you haven't used a pendulum before, try my ideas which you can adapt or discard when you create your own unique magical system. The rituals I have devised do work for many people but are intended only as a starting point for your own infinitely superior magic because it's about you, from you and for you.

Sometimes you may feel you want to use your Tarot cards, runes or playing cards to make a decision. But they don't seem to be making sense and are contradicting one another. The pendulum is remarkably good at untangling crossed divinatory wires and helping you to interpret the underlying meaning. If you have used any of the other Today's Woman magic systems, you will already have a basic general method whatever other form of divination you are using.

But however you have learned to use the runes, Tarot, playing cards, I Ching or crystals, you can use your pendulum to good effect with them.

If, for example, you are doing a Tarot reading and have nine cards in a spread that isn't making sense, then shuffle the original cards you chose and lay them face down in rows or a circle. Now move your pendulum over the cards from any direction until it gives the *'this one'* response over one card. Take that card and look at it and consider how its meaning relates to events in your life. You can ask the pendulum if you're not sure. Let the questions just come without thinking. The Tarot and pendulum are both expressions of your deep intuitive powers.

'Does this card refer to . . . ?'

If the answer is *'no'*, try a second question and if you get *'try-again',* then you will know

Pendulums with other forms of divination

there's a sticking point. In that case it may be helpful to choose a second card and see what that adds to the message. Remember that your interpretation of the cards or runes is as correct as anyone else's, so don't be tied to fixed meanings or methods once you have a basic idea of the symbols.

Then choose a second card with the pendulum and think about that, again asking questions if necessary. Add the third card and you'll have the heart of the original reading untangled and clear. If you want to add the remaining cards to the key three, you can use the pendulum to give you the order. But usually it isn't necessary after you have used the pendulum to find the key.

You can use your favourite divination system or learn one very easily — not for fortune-telling but to help you tune into the options on offer. I'll give you an example of how the pendulum was used with the Tarot cards, probably the easiest method to follow, even if you aren't familiar with the Tarot. I'm using the basic and very easy ideas I developed in *Tarot for Today's Woman*. But if you use a different method, your own meanings would be equally effective.

A Reading for Daphne
Daphne did a traditional ten card spread but could not make head nor tail of it. Rather than dashing off to the nearest clairvoyant for some professional advice, or heading for the drinks

cupboard, she turned to her clairvoyant on a string: her pendulum.

Daphne was convinced that the key lay within those ten cards and so she did not return them to the pack and start again. Instead she shuffled them and put them face down in a circle. This was the way she wanted to do it. But the magic would have worked if she'd put a card on each stone on the front path and danced round them in her frillies (though the logistics would have been harder). Daphne passed the pendulum slowly around the circle of cards until it stopped.

She turned the chosen card over. It was the **Sun,** the traditional card of fire and light and, in the *Today's Woman* system, a card very much associated with our potential, the things we still want to do but have never had or made the chance for.

While trying to make sense of her cards en masse Daphne had missed the deep personal significance of the **Sun**. She wanted to take an Open University course though she was coming up to retirement. But her grown-up children said it was ridiculous as she was too old to start a new career and would be nearly seventy when she got her honours degree.

So should she go for it? The next card was the **Empress** and that, in anyone's language, is Mother Earth: supportive, caring, thinking of others and getting a bit fed up with helping

A reading for Daphne

lame ducks. This turns up in a remarkable number of readings that I do for older women who are heading for the sunset when their former free-wheeling teenagers hit forty, turn traditional and remind mum she should be home babysitting not gadding about. (Remember that this happened to Claire when she wanted to retire to Normandy. The outer quadrants of the options cloth told her to take practical steps — big ones across the Channel.)

The **Empress** was significant in reminding Daphne that she'd done her share of living for others and that she wanted to do the degree for herself and not to benefit anyone else.

The third choice was unerring, the **Hierophant** who's tied up with guilt and convention and what we've been brought up to feel is our duty. He often turns up with the **Empress** in tow.

And although Daphne denied it at first (the appearance of the **Hierophant** usually heralds an immediate denial because he's a clever chap and hides in the recesses of our mind), deep down she had been feeling that maybe she was being selfish.

But of course she is less likely to be a burden to her kids in the future if she makes a life of her own (she is a widow) and does not try to live through them. After that Daphne could see how the other cards fitted in. But they weren't really necessary for she was off to buy her books for her course.

I'd suggest you start with the Major Arcana Tarot (the first 22 numbered cards in the pack) as this is the most accessible if you have no prior knowledge of the system. The Major Arcana meanings are based on symbols that have been with us since the dawn of Time and will still be relevant when we use robots to shuffle the deck. They are the mother, father, the child (or fool) the wise man (hermit) etc.

The Major Arcana

Pick out nine cards from a shuffled pack without looking and lay them face down (you could use your pendulum to make your selection from the full pack but it could take an age — however, if you have the time on your hands then don't let me discourage you).

Dowse over the selected nine until you feel drawn to three of them. Then interpret the meanings according to whatever images come into your head.

This was the original way of reading the oracle of the I Ching. It sprang from looking at the cracks on a roasted tortoise shell and deciphering the images of a river or clouds or whatever.

In fact, my own book on the I Ching went back to the original images without the endless layers of obscure interpretations plastered on them by generations of scholars.

However, if you are feeling low on inspiration you can base your ideas on these mini-

The Major Arcana

definitions of the cards which are taken from my book, *Tarot Divination for Today's Woman*.

The Fool tells you to trust your intuition rather than the wisdom of others.

The Magician involves making the first step towards a new venture.

The High Priestess talks of doing your own thing.

The Empress is the Mother Earth figure that can find you weighed down with the cares of others.

The Emperor represents the achievements that you make in the real world. Don't let others put you down.

The Hierophant involves old guilts that you need to shed to move forward.

The Lovers card talks about relationships and seeing people for what they really are.

Justice says that you should deal with petty injustices before they build up.

The Hermit tells you to withdraw from a no-win situation and listen to your inner voice.

The Wheel of Fortune advises you to find the best solution rather than leaving fate to solve your problems.

Strength reminds you of your inner strengths and says that you should stick to your guns.

The Hanged Man is the card of accepting life the way it is and discarding unrealistic dreams.

Death is the card of natural change and says we must be ready to move on.

Temperance deals with peace of mind and letting old resentments go.

The Devil is the card of negative emotions. Acknowledge yours.

The Tower of Destruction talks about freeing yourself from old restrictions.

The Star says there are many dreams that you can still fulfil if you believe in yourself.

The Moon is the card of the easy path and the illusion that it is better to accept the way things are.

The Sun is the card of your hidden talents that you might never have used.

Judgment advises you to forgive yourself for any mistakes and assess whether others are being fair to you.

The World is the card of moving forward confident that you are on the right track.

Day

24

The Minor
Arcana

But supposing you want to use playing cards or the Minor Arcana where you can't guess so easily at basic meanings, even with a pictorial set. You could buy a simple divinatory book and look up relevant meanings each time for the cards the pendulum picks.

It really is worthwhile learning one particular system, although you will find that they all have many common factors. In the meantime, I'll suggest a few basic definitions from my own series.

These definitions aren't meant to be learned unless you've got a photographic memory but are just for your reference. If you are using the Tarot these only apply to the numbered cards of the Minor Arcana.

I'll deal with the court cards another day, so for now you might want to remove them when you make your selection.

Initially you can get much information by simply looking at the suit of the card the pendulum has picked out and you may want to ignore the actual value of the card.

Again pick nine cards at random from the shuffled pack and dowse over those for three. See if any suit predominates or if they are fairly evenly divided. This will tell you whether you need to concentrate on one particular issue or whether you need to keep your options open and be prepared to adapt. Next look at which

suit or suits are missing and ask the pendulum
why.

Diamonds in the playing cards or **Pentacles** in
the Tarot are to do with the practical issues of
living. If you feel bogged down look for a
practical solution. Be prepared for a bit of
slog to achieve your goal.

Hearts in the playing cards and **Cups** in the
Tarot are to do with relationships at home
and at work. Try to understand what people
really mean and if in doubt about the wisdom
of a venture follow your gut feeling.

Clubs or **Wands** are to do with you personally
and all those ideas and dreams you have. Go
for what you can achieve and use your inspiration to see you through the obstacles.

Spades or **Swords** are talking about the has-
sles that usually arise, not out of bad luck or
malicious fate, but from our own oversights
or inaction in the past. The way forward lies
in logic and swift decisive action, not hot air.

You can get a good idea of what a card is
talking about by concentrating on the suit. But
to get extra information you can note the
number as well as the suit that your pendulum
chooses.

If it chooses a particular number more than
once e.g. three threes or two sixes, then it's an
issue to be looked at carefully.

Divining by numbers   Again, let your pendulum choose three out of nine Minor Arcana or ordinary playing cards that you have picked from the pack at random. Leave out the Court cards at this stage.

You do not have to memorise the values before moving on, although you might want to write them in your divination diary for quick reference.

The Aces in playing card divination or the Tarot represent a beginning or an unexpected change of plan or attitude and are positive, creative cards.

The Twos in both systems are to do with balancing events or calls on your time or with partnership issues, whether in love or business.

The Threes talk of moving forward in the real world and giving form to ideas though this may involve a great deal of input with no immediate reward in sight.

The Fours are the cards of limiting ourselves by holding on to partial achievement or happiness, or looking back to where we know it is safe. Sometimes we need to consider whether it's better to go for broke or opt for security.

The Fives are the cards of restlessness, regretting what we haven't done or feeling discontented with the people and material. But used positively the fives can be a great impetus for action.

The Sixes are the cards of idealism where principles matter more than ambition or success. But sometimes we forget to keep earthly matters going.

The Sevens are the cards of the inner world and happiness within ourselves. But we need to beware of illusion and opting out.

The Eights are the cards of taking practical steps towards a goal, whether moving on in a physical way or learning a new skill.

The Nines are the cards of personal achievement and happiness that may involve great courage and effort at a time when we may feel we've reached our limit.

The Tens talk about the completion of a phase or ambition in our lives often involving others which may bring great happiness but is also an ending of a particular phase.

Day
25

If you are especially concerned with people and relationships, then you can use either the sixteen court cards of the Minor Arcana or the twelve Court cards in a normal deck for a reading with your pendulum. Or, of course, you can simply add them to your pack and see if the pendulum picks them. Remember there are sixteen court cards in the Tarot (the **Jack**

The Court Cards

The Court Cards

of the playing card pack is split into the **Page** and **Knight**) as opposed to twelve in the playing card system.

Whether you are using the Court cards alone or the Minor Arcana, make your random selection of nine cards (or, if you have the time, dowse over the cards and see which you are drawn to). Place them face down and see which three the pendulum chooses. Don't feel you have to learn the definitions off by heart before you try this.

The Jacks and the **Pages** and **Knights** in the Tarot can refer to people in our lives, but often they highlight a particular stage or area where we are looking to other people to help us along. Don't worry about the difference between **Page** and **Knight** in this quickie guide as it's really only one of degree. Both these cards are telling us that we may have to trust our own instincts more than we trust the wisdom of other people.

The Queens are the opposite and talk about the way we can occupy a central role in other people's lives. This can be very creative but, if you are finding this a strain, ask yourself if your constant support is really necessary.

The Kings talk about power and competitiveness, so they are very good cards for women in a man's world, so long as we don't forget to use our feminine intuitive abilities as well.

You're feeling out of sorts, tired, nauseous, bloated. It may be that time of the month when you can barely resist savaging the bus conductor, who rings the bell before you're on the platform and sends shopping, papers and your aching body cascading over the nearest seats. Telling you that it's PMT is less than useless. What you want is to feel better. But how?

Pendulums and health

Or suppose your stress level is in overdrive so that you are writing reports in your head, or arguing with an absent lover as dawn breaks and you begin each day looking like the supporting role in a horror movie. Who can help?

How about your pendulum for starters? We know that the pain we feel in one area may be symptomatic of disorder elsewhere and if it's a stress problem then it reverberates though every tensed muscle. So what we're dowsing for is not just the trouble spot — you've probably got a shrewd idea about that already — but for the root of the problem and most importantly for the remedy to 'ease the dis-ease'.

The pendulum is especially useful for your own problems. You don't need any formal training for, as with every other function of the pendulum, it's driven by your needs and your inner knowledge.

It's also very good with your own children's ailments. They accept quite happily that pendulums are magic and so their inner selves cooperate wonderfully. If, however, you want to

Pendulums and health help others on a regular basis, then it's best to contact a healing association for advice and training (see useful addresses at the back).

If you are in the pink and emanating vitality from every pore, then you can ignore the next few sections till you feel off-colour, unless you would like to read them through for future reference.

If you do have a physical problem, however trivial it seems to the outside world, decide which is the worst physical symptom and hold your pendulum over the affected area. You might need help with your back but ask a sympathetic friend rather than an 'expert' who may impose her diagnosis on you.

And as for the average male, ten to one his retarded sense of humour will suggest a bit of 'healing nooky'.

Ask the pendulum if where you feel the pain is the source of the real problem? If it says *'yes'*, then you can go on to finding the cause. If not you'll need to move the pendulum round until you get a *'yes'* response.

Don't be surprised if your back pain is located primarily in your head. You are not being a hypochondriac but your stress levels may be causing you to sleep less and to hold your body like a taut bow-string. You might like to make a flow chart for more complex healing matters as you did for divination.

For today, let the pendulum move to the areas of pain or discomfort and visualise warm golden light flowing into the afflicted bits. Or, if you feel generally awful, move the pendulum round your body instinctively following the energy patterns.

Remember that people can successfully dowse from a map so you don't have to move your pendulum in any set physical way to make contact.

Healing Rituals
Even if you are feeling on top of the world a bit of healing light won't go amiss though you might like to think of someone who is unhappy or ill and share the light with them.

Indeed, if you can develop your own healing rituals you will find they are especially effective for you, though maybe not for others.

If the traditional Eastern idea of energy centres (known as *chakras*) is valid for you, then you can direct your pendulum over them. But if you do not understand or do not like the concept, then concentrate on feeling the warmth and healing and don't worry about whether you're 'doing it correctly'. As I keep stressing, what is important is what is valid for you.

You are unique and so should respond in your own unique fashion to what you instinctively feel. After all, animals learn very few of their healing rituals by observation. Much comes

Healing rituals

naturally, as you will have seen if you have ever reared an orphaned kitten or puppy.

Now have a warm bath and an early night. Feed the kids a picnic, paper plates and all and make them a quiet den in their room so they can have a peaceful evening and leave you to yours. (I keep emergency supplies of colouring books, crayons and story audio tapes hidden away to dole out to my kids when I want to preserve my peace of mind.)

If you're still hyped up, try listening to some tapes of those songs that recall those golden nights at the Locarno when you were the Twinkle of Walsall or the Belle of Brixton. Tonight you should forget about that phone call to mum or those letters that you really ought to write.

And if the old man wants to carry on chewing over yesterday's hassle, don't rise to the bait. Let him have a happy few hours crowing. You can shoot him down in flames tomorrow if you still feel aggrieved, but probably you won't. Forget about the niggles with neighbours or flatmates and leave the troubles at work behind for a few hours.

Hang your pendulum at the end of your bed or put it on the bedside table, close your eyes and be wherever you want to be. And that might even be absolutely nowhere except cocooned in soft cotton-wool clouds.

Usually you'll go on to discover the cause of your problems as soon as you've located the source. So rediscover your source of trouble. Maybe the early night and nice dreams dispersed it.

Or the pain or tension may have shifted. If so, go to the new place of friction. Now ask the pendulum a few questions about what the pain is saying, because discomfort is usually a signal to slow down or get help. So a sensible first question would be: is the problem mainly a physical one?

A 'yes'/'no' health check

If the pendulum's response is *'yes'*, then you need to know if time will cure it. A remarkable number of physical ills do disappear of their own accord and a little more rest and some of the tender loving care you dish out to others may be all you need.

If the pendulum says that time is not the answer, then do you need to seek professional help? If the answer is *'yes'*, then you can consult your GP (if your doctor is a traditionalist be a bit vague as to how you came across your information).

With acute or sudden illnesses in young children it's as well to err on the side of caution as every mum knows. But the maternal instinct can often detect more serious problems that need intervention before they flare up. Indeed, the pendulum gives us a distinctive sign of this automatic maternal radar that is very different from free-floating anxiety, which can actually be lowered by using the instincts tapped by the pendulum.

If in your own case the pendulum says that the remedy does not lie in seeking professional advice, then you can ask if you can make an adjustment to your life that will remedy the ill. And so you can go on with questions about diet, etc. If you get the *'try-again'* response, then you may need to see what is the sticking point and rephrase the question.

However, the pendulum may say that it's not mainly a physical problem. In this case you need to question it in order to locate the source of the stress. Then you can either put it right, or accept it's something you have to live with and take up meditation or find tactics to help you cope. Again, the pendulum will help you to discover which.

All this is quite easy using your pendulum's *'yes'/'no'/'try again'* mechanism, especially if you add a flow chart when the going gets complex.

A Reading for Amanda

Amanda had frequent blinding migraines but tablets not only failed to help but actually left her feeling worse. First she ran her pendulum round her body and ended with it vibrating over her stomach. Thinking she'd got it wrong she asked the pendulum: *Is my head the source of my migraine?*

No.

Are my eyes the source of my migraine?

No.

Is my stomach the source of my migraine?

Yes.

(The pendulum is remarkably patient).

Is the cause of my migraine mainly physical?

Yes.

Do I need to seek professional help?

No.

Does the answer lie in my lifestyle?

Yes.

Is it my diet at fault?

Yes.

Amanda was puzzled. She's one of those people who never buys chocolate or pigs out on dairy products or refined wheat. And she also knew that the migraines were not hormonal because they occurred only every couple of months and at different times in her menstrual cycle.

A reading for Amanda

So then she asked:

Is it something I eat only just before an attack?

Yes.

Is it something I buy or cook?

No.

Is it something I eat when I am at home?

No.

Is it something I eat when I'm at work?

No.

Then she realised the truth in one of those intuitive leaps that hit us in the eye. She always got an attack the day after she'd visited her boyfriend's mum, which was about every eight weeks. And they got on well so it wasn't one of those sneaky tension illnesses which can masquerade as an allergy.

Yet Amanda stuck to her normal diet except for some biscuits. Her boyfriend's mother made some rather sticky, gorgeous biscuits containing fruit and spices and 'a secret ingredient'.

Is it the biscuits?

Yes.

The next time that Amanda went to see her boyfriend's mother she pretended she was on a diet. Amanda has not discovered the ingredient she was allergic to as this is one of those closely-guarded secret family recipes. But her health has improved dramatically.

Day 28

A Well-being cloth

As with other forms of divination, a permanent cloth may be useful for looking at health matters that may involve more than one underlying factor. Find another old scarf or a piece of cloth a foot to eighteen inches square and your indelible marker.

Draw round a saucer or make a circle about this size. This inner circle is the area of *physical* or organic well-being.

The pendulum will respond here if the root of the problem is a physical one, for sometimes what we blame on stress can have a simple and often curable physical component. Getting to know our body rhythms, strengths and weaknesses can give us a head start in life and while we cannot and should not change our basic bodily structure, sensible weight loss or gain and keeping ourselves fit can maximise our physical potential.

After you've drawn this circle do something to improve your physical well-being whether going for a swim, cycle ride or walk, enrolling for a physical activity whether bowls or aerobics, treating yourself to a massage or even

A Well-being cloth throwing out all those additive-loaded snacks that perhaps, like me, you've squirrelled away for the next rainy day.

Draw round a tea plate or make a circle about this size. This is the middle circle, the area of *mental* well-being.

If the pendulum responds here, the root of your problem is stress. For worry, repressed anger or anxiety can, as you know only too well, lead to insomnia, over-eating or drinking, or lack of appetite, a constant racing heart and pulse and muscle pain from being constantly poised for flight or fight.

If we didn't feel stress we'd not have the impetus to move so channeled into the right sources it can be positive. Tension can also lead to depression and lethargy and the vicious circle of feeling helpless and being unable to do anything about it.

When you've drawn this circle do something to improve or maintain your mental well-being. Contact friends who make you feel good. Save the moaning minnies and nit-pickers for another day or cut them out of your life where possible to keep yourself feeling on top form.

If you're the one feeling aggrieved, then talk to a friend who is mutually supportive and get it off your chest followed by a good laugh or cry about the problem. If you're alone, then

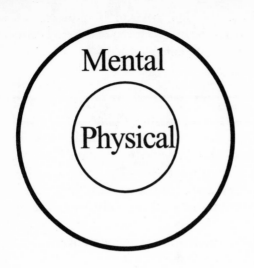

have a loud yell or pillow thump. Then put on some music and sing and dance around — if you've young kids let them join in the dancing bit—they don't need practice at yelling. To the over-eights, as mothers know to their cost, such maternal aberrations are so uncool as to be off the clock and today is a time for feeling harmonious. So it's worth a pound to get rid of them for an hour while you lower your tension level.

You may find that the pendulum is drawn to both circles as physical ills can result from a combination of organic and environmental sources, in which case you need to look to both areas.

After you've dowsed over the inner two circles you'll know where the problem resides. But the third outermost circle is vital in finding a more permanent remedy than the ones I've suggested.

Day

29

The outer circle of resolution

Draw round a dinner plate or make a circle about this size. The outer circle is the area of *resolution* or *remedy*.

Now divide the outer circle only into four, with lines at the 12, 3, 6 and 9 o'clock positions. In the Well-being cloth unlike the divination cloth I'm not using the outer quadrants, only the three circles.

The 12-3 o'clock quadrant represents *letting nature take its course*. Remember that, as I said earlier, you can help matters along by getting plenty of rest, eating a sensible diet and avoiding unnecessary stress — for starters friends or relatives who thrive on making you feel guilty or inadequate.

The 3-6 o'clock quadrant is the *seek expert advice* area either from your GP or alternative practitioner, maybe both. It's worthwhile finding practitioners you do trust well in advance as professional compatibility is important in getting the most from a consultation, especially if when you are feeling vulnerable.

The 6-9 o'clock quadrant is the area of *Environmental change*. If it is a stress problem, then maybe you need to sort out the issue that's

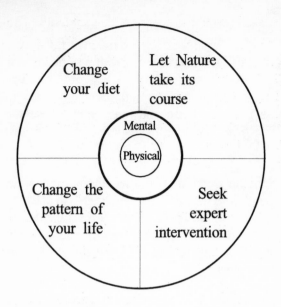

keeping you awake. But if you cannot sort it out, then perhaps you could practise relaxation or try to develop other more positive areas in your life to compensate.

If you felt a physical response in the innermost circle, look at issues such as smokers at work who are clogging your lungs, or overlong hours on a VDU. See whether you can improve your working environment by negotiation, either with management or your colleagues.

The 9-12 o'clock quadrant concentrates on *Dietary Issues*, since this is a prime candidate for all kinds of dis-ease both mental and physical in our lives. You may be allergic to certain foods or simply eating too much of the wrong kind of food and too little of the right sort. Or you may be taking too much alcohol or additives. Since food is sometimes an emotive and deep-seated issue you may need to use the *'yes'/'no'/'try-again'* responses of your pendulum.

In the quadrants of the outer circle, your pendulum may be drawn to more than one area if a combination of factors are implicated in your dis-ease. Try changes in the relevant practical sphere and see what improvements take place.

I haven't suggested any specific remedies because you will probably have your own well-tried and tested ones. Or, if you're new to homeopathic remedies and want to try them, then it's best either to consult a reliable practitioner initially (contact addresses are given at the back of the book), or to go down to your local health store. Your local pharmacist is often a fund of information in conventional medicine and may well be a first port of call.

Day 30

The cloth in action

A Reading for Suzy

Suzy has three small children and from time to time is troubled by excruciating back pain and difficulty in movement. Her Quasimodo impersonation, when she bends down and cannot straighten up again, delights the children, but is no joke when she has to do the school run as well as organise a party plan business from home.

Suzy doesn't need to find the source of her pain and previous visits to the doctor have resulted in yet another bottle of painkillers that seem less and less effective. The doctor says it's a disc problem and that physiotherapy can't help at this stage, while surgery is a bit drastic.

The pendulum, not surprisingly, went to the inner circle of *physical well-being*. Suzy could remember the original injury- trying to move a heavy settee alone some years before. So she tried dowsing over the remedy quadrants and the pendulum then went straight to diet.

'I know that,' Suzy laughed. 'I'm a yo-yo dieter and when I get to a certain maximum weight my back "goes" and then I embark on another diet.'

So Suzy really knew the answer. In fact, her doctor had grumbled about her weight on several occasions. He had offered her a strict diet sheet that she kept to for a few days but quickly abandoned. Although there was no magic cure for her back problem, it was certain that dieting would help.

That's not magic, I can hear the yells. She already knew that. But then nine times out of ten we all really know the answers the pendulum gives. They come from within us and not some wisdom from beyond. What the pendu-

lum helps us to do is to cut through to the —
sometimes very bitter — truth which our conscious mind tries to block out when it is too
painful.

But although Suzy knew the solution, she still
had her back problems because she wasn't
applying the remedy — at least not properly.
Until we act upon our knowledge in an effective way we may be left with the original
problem.

So back to the pendulum. Suzy remembered
to ask questions spontaneously to catch her
conscious mind out when it was blocking the
truth. Why wasn't her dieting permanently
successful?

Am I sabotaging my own efforts to be slim?

Yes.

Am I setting myself unrealistic targets?

Yes.

Suzy protested but then realised that she
always stopped dieting when she'd lost a couple of stones which was enough to stop the back
trouble, but far short of the model girl target
she'd set herself. And so in her own eyes she'd
failed and gave up. Then she started putting on
weight and the back trouble recurred.

So the next question was:

Do I want to be really slim?

No.

It doesn't matter why Suzy doesn't want to
have a perfect figure. The important point is
that she accepts that for her, a couple of stone
represents a realistic and attainable target. So
she's trying the pendulum instead of the scales.

Some people get very indignant when the
pendulum, or any other divinatory form, suggests that they should do something that they
are already doing. But often the very reason
this message pops up is because any attempts
at following the plan are only half-hearted. In
such cases, as with Suzy, it's important to look
at why the efforts fall short and if perhaps we
are asking something unreasonable of ourselves. Or it may be that deep down we don't
really want the change we are supposed to be
seeking and so sabotage our own efforts. But
that's another story.

Now try a Well-being reading either using
your cloth or drawing the circles on paper. If
you are well balanced right now, your pendulum won't react at all to any of the categories.
So you can put your cloth away for a rainy day
and go out and enjoy the sunshine in your life.

You may find, like Suzy, that once your cloth
has located the relevant areas you might like to
pinpoint remedies by adding the *'yes'/'no'*
method.

Pendulum healing

You can use your pendulum to send light and warmth to heal yourself and your children, for they were once part of your body. You could even try with your own mum.

Your field of positive psychic power is strongest for those you are connected to physically. Healing others, whether by contact or at a distance, involves considerable psychic and spiritual energy. And you do need to be aware of what you are doing and how to control your powers so that you're not buzzing all night. If you do want to try this then it's best to contact a reputable organisation for training (see the back of the book for useful addresses).

However, anyone can send love and light to others and the pendulum is a good way of doing this. Go somewhere quiet and light a candle, white for creative energy, pink for reconciliation, purple for spirituality or blue for the higher accesses of the mind.

Hold your pendulum so that it feels comfortable and think of those you love who are unhappy or ill and, as you blow out your candle, send your loving thoughts to them.

If you feel negatively towards someone who has wronged you, then send them love and light too. Who knows? You may get a nice letter or phone-call in return. Even if you don't, at least you've replaced your own negativity with positive action and can move on to the next phase in your life unencumbered.

Many people have glimpses of previous existences and even though these may not be verifiable they can shed light on present dilemmas. Your pendulum can help you to glimpse this other dimension of experience without needing to be hypnotised.

Even with reliable regression therapists — and the profession has more than its share of over-enthusiastic amateurs and charlatans — the danger in approaching past memories through a third party is that he or she may, albeit unconsciously, influence and colour your perceptions.

Find a quiet time and light blue candles for your mind or purple for your spirit or silver the colour of the moon and the unconscious world. Swirl your pendulum round if it's a crystal one so that it catches the light. You can also do this in the early morning sun or by sunlit water.

Let the pictures form in your mind as you sit on your rainbow swirling carousel or shadowy world of candlelight. Don't try to analyse them, just watch them as you would a kaleidoscope or magic lantern.

Afterwards you might like to write a few words, perhaps a poem or a story. You could even paint or draw your impressions. Whatever you produce, keep it in your ring folder because such things are private and precious and not for the analysis of others. Be patient and don't expect full-blown scenarios. You are more likely to get just flashes of colour, even a sudden scent or unexpected sound from far away.

Or you might like to hold your pendulum over a map of your locality, or even further afield if you've a holiday coming up. See if any places give an echo of meaning for you. Tempting though it is to imagine yourself as a Hawaiian maiden or Pharaoh's daughter, the pendulum is just as likely to land on Bognor or Basildon. If you feel strongly drawn to a place, go there and see if you're attracted to a particular building. This need not necessarily be a stately home. It could be a disused factory, mill or even a row of old terraced cottages.

If you can't travel far, ask your pendulum if it can suggest a similar location nearer to home. Your pendulum may find hints in your immediate area of another more distant place that strikes chords of familiarity, like an extended and enriched form of déjà vu that you may develop in dreams and day-time visions.

Just let your pendulum take you where it will and don't try to force memories. You could even go down to a big bus or train station if you've plenty of time and see which train or bus your pendulum chooses. Get a Rover ticket so you can get on and off.

At worst you'll get a fun day out. But you may find a new depth and meaning to seemingly unrelated feelings or preferences. If you can't afford even the price of a ticket to the town centre, let your pendulum choose the direction you walk or cycle. For every past memory that involves India or Egypt, there are dozens more that seem to be much closer to home. Many would-be Rajahs or Mandarins in their past lives may find clearer echoes of home in an inner city area.

But if you are strongly drawn to long past exotica and nothing else will do, try the British Museum or the Museum of Mankind in London where you can find American Indian, African, Chinese and Egyptian artefacts. This is where a pendant pendulum is invaluable. Visit these museums near opening or closing times, when you won't get hordes of school parties using work-sheets as missiles and tearing round in record time to reach the shop.

A bit of advance research can uncover all manner of historical relics in your location or Industrial Museum. If possible, go for the real thing and not a reconstructed Tudor village complete with canned minstrel music. A British Heritage or National Trust card can open many doors to the past for you and your pendulum to explore.

One women I corresponded with found a Canadian totem pole that she felt strong links with at Virginia Water in Surrey.

Of course you can explore past lives without a pendulum but it can be very reassuring to see its familiar movement to confirm what you feel in your heart. It's unlikely you'll get enough material to star in a documentary on Channel Four. But what matters is that you can understand why you feel strongly about an apparently unimportant scenario in your present life and pull together what may have seemed seem illogical strands in your life.

Day 33

Pendulums and trust

Can you trust Mr or Ms Too Good to Be True or someone who comes up with the offer of a lifetime?

I'm not suggesting you dangle your pendulum over every guy before you accept a date or astound your bank manager by openly dowsing over the overdraft offer that seems to tie you and your heirs to the bank till Judgment Day.

But women do have strong gut feelings about people and contracts that are invariably right. In the anxiety of the moment however it's easy to doubt yourself and go along with conventional wisdom or seeming expertise to your cost.

So how can you use your pendulum in crunch situations without shaking confidence in others as to your credit worthiness in love or money?

Of course, it is possible to pull out your pendulum while you are on the telephone to

It is possible to pull out your pendulum while you are on the phone to someone

someone and dowse for a *'yes'/'no'* response to the question in the back of your mind: 'Can I trust this character?' But how can you do it in plan sight?

As you get to know your pendulum you'll find that it will respond with little perceptible movement. Instead of letting it swing, hold the pendulum itself and you will feel quite a strong current or vibration for the *'yes'* response and a different sort or buzzing or even nothing for *'no'*.

You can ask your pendulum to show you the difference in advance and if you're worried whether or not you've got it right, start using your pendulum to confirm 'off the top of your head' or 'gut' decisions on issues that aren't so vital at first. Then you'll have the confidence to trust it in important issues.

Pendulums and trust

If you're wearing a pendulum pendant there's no problem — you can just touch it gently as you speak. Or you might like to carry a small pendulum or personal charm in your pocket or bag that you can hold, out of sight, while you are making an important decision with other people present.

This will provide you with an excellent independent checker at times when you suspect that the allegedly trustworthy characters are really blinding you with science or doublespeak.

This outer sign of our inner conviction can be vital in giving us the confidence to go it alone if necessary. You may hear your inner voice loud and clear, or feel a dig in the pit of your stomach which your pendulum will gently but persistently echo.

If not, then whatever you are being told about the urgency of any situation, usually the offer of a lifetime can be put on hold for a few minutes, if not longer (unless, like Cinderella, your meter runs out at midnight). Go for a walk to think things over if you can. Or you can even escape to the loo.

If you can't get away physically — if, for example, you are trapped in the bank manager's officer — stall for time by asking the other person to explain some detail. Or you can let them talk about themselves while you move far away in your head where you can hear your real inner voice and that of your pendulum.

Back in the old days the wise woman of the village swung a needle over the womb of a pregnant woman to determine the sex of the unborn baby. You can do the same using your pendulum. Dangle it over your womb and ask the all important question.

Day
34

Pendulums and pregnancy

However, during my research into the psychic links between mothers and children (for my book *A Mother's Instincts*) found that 90 per cent of women knew the sex of their unborn child. In many cases, what stops a woman from knowing the sex exactly is the pressure that comes from outside. This is usually a partner or relatives who want us to have a boy or a girl, instead of just accepting that we are giving birth to a child and that is the important thing.

Their expectations cloud our own inner visions and it is nice if the pendulum can confirm what we suspect deep down. Then we can tell Aunt Agatha that it is no good her knitting little pink sleeping suits, or tell hubby that he will have to put the football boots away until the next time.

You may want to lend your pendulum to any expectant friend (or buy one as an early birthday present). Let her establish her own *'yes'/'no'* response. If she gets a *'try-again'*, there may be more than one inmate in her womb! It really is best if the pregnant woman does it herself as a third party can get in the way of mother/foetus dialogue.

Pendulums and pregnancy

If you are pregnant yourself, then your pendulum can alert you to the moment of conception. Many women do know this already but the *'yes'* response from your pendulum can help, especially if the issue's clouded with anxieties.

You can even try using your pendulum to alert you to the time you're particularly fertile. Some women have a barely perceptible physical sensation at ovulation and some women even have dreams. But those of us who have a less tangible sense of awareness, find that the days, or even hours, of peak fertility are detectable only by an instinctive gut reaction which it's easy to distrust.

Of course there are no guarantees and there is no substitute for medical help if there is a physical block to conception.

But for some couples, anxiety can be an unwanted contraceptive. At least producing a crystal pendulum is more romantic than getting out the thermometer and ovulation chart before deciding if it's time for a romantic dinner for two or a jog round the park.

You can even talk to your baby via the pendulum. Lie quietly and ask the baby questions while dangling the pendulum over your womb.

For the unborn child's psyche and yours are very close and it is a magical time when the boundaries of possibility are at their widest.

The psychic pendulum is remarkably useful in everyday life. I wouldn't suggest that you went as far as my middle son Jack's attempts to use it as a can-opener. Jack was struggling to open a carton of drink when, without warning, he seized the pointed crystal pendulum I was wearing round my neck and plunged it into the top of his drink. Next minute pendulum and I were showered in blackcurrant juice. 'Oh, sorry mummy,' said Jack and trotted off happily clutching his drink!

Practical pendulum power

But the pendulum is very good at helping you to find what you've lost. As I said before, I don't believe practical dowsing is a skill to be rehearsed with little exercises. Indeed, you are unlikely to succeed if your friend has hidden your car keys in your muddy wellies and is hooting with laughter as you search among the geraniums. This can cause you to doubt your ability which, at its roots, rests on trusting your instincts in real life.

Wait till you're about to drive the kids to school for their annual trip and you're running late. Elder daughter points out as you coax the engine into life that youngest son is wearing only his socks.

Undeterred by your anguished yelps the kids begin demolishing their packed lunch in the back seat while Postman Pat from the tape player grinds down the faltering battery even further. The thought of having to keep the kids at home all day or worse still drive them at top speed to Chessington Zoo to catch up with the coach can push your dowsing abilities into top gear.

When panic hits, hold the pendulum and walk. Don't think consciously of the most likely place for the hidden object. You know there's no chance of it being there. The pendulum may either swing in the direction it wants you to go or keep the *'yes'* response going till you hit gold, or whatever you'd give a Sultan's treasure to find at that particular moment.

If you've got a bit longer or the panic isn't great and doubts creep in, pick up your pendulum and as you do so concentrate on thinking backwards. There's no rule that says you can't use psychology as well when the odds are stacked against you. Let me take you on a typical family scavenger hunt.

Five-year-old Bill has lost his school bag. He came out of school with it in the afternoon, dumped it in the back of the car. Sixteen hours later it's vanished. I ignore the suggestions that his toy dinosaur has eaten it. He got out of the car. Now was it with or without the bag?

I can't remember and my children who can recite every word of dialogue of their favourite cartoons backwards look as though I've asked them to reveal the secrets of the Holy Grail. Resisting the desire to throttle the nearest child with the pendulum I ask the pendulum:

Is the missing bag in the car?

No.

Correct so far. Bill had his new Batman car inside the bag and wanted to play with it. But I wouldn't let him get the toy out while we were in the car as he would bop his sister with it who was winding him up as usual. So, as he wanted the toy, he would have brought the bag in with him instead of dropping it in the car as he usually does.

Is the bag in the house?

No.

Is the bag in the garden?

Yes.

More weary neurons burst into life as recollection dawns. Pausing only to grab a peanut butter sandwich, Bill had headed for the garden with his bag waving round his head like Roy Rogers' lasso. I told him off, but was distracted by my daughter treading on a Lego brick and screaming as though her leg had been amputated, before I could tell him to put the bag down. I double check with the pendulum.

Is the Batman car still in the bag?

Yes.

Practical pendulum power

We're hot on the trail. Bill got diverted from getting the car out of the bag because he found a frog on the path. He'd asked me if he could take it to school for his teacher and I'd delivered a mini-environmental lecture. He must have dropped the bag when he picked up the frog. Pendulum and I are moving in haste towards the pond.

On the way I ask if it's in the pond.

Pendulum reassures me it's not. Maybe it's being kind.

Is the bag near the pond?

Yes.

Guided by the pendulum swing I'm heading in the direction of the shed. Psychic twenty questions is losing its charm. Is it in the shed? Can it be hiding among all those abandoned bits of furniture, mice, wood lice and worse? No, says the pendulum, but we're still heading shed-wards according to its swing.

Is it behind the shed?

Yuk. Behind the shed makes the inside qualify for Good Housekeeping. I wonder whether I should have tried remote dowsing from the front room with a stiff drink.

No.

Pendulum veers sharply and I almost trip over Bill's pedal car with the lift-up seat.

Eureka. I lift the seat of the pedal car and there is Bill's school bag. I remove the wood lice and we're on our way. The Batman car is still inside. What about the reading book that had started the search in the first place? That wasn't in the bag. Bill informed me he'd left it at school!

Day 36

Dowsing without a pendulum

Can you dowse without a pendulum? Yes. Kath, the daughter of a close friend, can tell anyone where they've put anything. For example she recently went to a house for the first time and her new acquaintance wanted to show Kath a photo album but couldn't find it.

'On the second shelf above the dressing table in the spare bedroom,' Kath told her automatically.

That took some explaining. Kath has had the ability from a child and her mum phones her up if she can't find her keys or cheque book. Another Uri Geller? No, because Kath insists there's nothing psychic about her ability and gets very annoyed if anyone comments on it. Her mum is a professional clairvoyant but the 'amateur' leads the way in the finding field.

But for most of us, especially if we doubt our intuitive abilities, the pendulum is a way of cutting corners and focusing on the search a step at a time, rather than running round in circles like a demented road runner yelling at everyone.

So I won't be volunteering to demonstrate my pendulum skills on TV. Like a lot of women my psyche is fired mainly by crisis and I've enough of those in real life.

I'd love to hear readers' success stories which I'll include in my next book on the subject.

Day 37

There are cases of people who've successfully used dowsing to find lost humans and, assuming that the person wants to be found, if you keep calm then a pendulum may help. I'm not talking about those awful cases when children get taken away.

Finding lost animals

Here, your need to find the child is compounded by fear and grief and, as a mother who has lost my very adventurous children briefly on occasions for less sinister reasons, I can't imagine how the overwhelming emotion could leave space for any other instincts. Perhaps this is why so few parents can link in with missing children.

I've come across cases where parents send love to a distressed child a long way off but that's a different story. In *A Mother's Instincts* I tell how a young man called 'Help mum' when he overturned his car in a snowy ditch.

Miles away his mother picked up his distress. Alastair somehow found the strength to right the car, get it back on the road and arrived home shocked, but relatively unhurt.

Even if you can't manage such superhuman feats by psychic power, it's not too difficult to find a lost cat or dog using a pendulum or even by pure intuition. And cats and dogs can do it too. Clementine the cat was owned by an American woman who left her with friends when she moved home, as Clementine was heavily pregnant.

However, Clementine had other ideas and travelled more than 1,600 miles across the great plains from Dunkirk, New York to Denver in Colorado to find her owner. The cat was identified by seven toes on each forepaw, two unmistakeable white blotches in her stomach and a scar on her left shoulder where she'd been singed by hot coals.

This takes us back to the unknown aspects because the cat had never been to her new home.

It's also said that stags in the northern wastes dowse with their antlers for suitable spots to lure the females in droves. Perhaps that's what the boys were doing hanging round the door of the Locarno ballroom during my youth.

If you are quiet and calm, you may well be able to trace a pet using the instinctive power of

Finding lost animals your pendulum. Don't expect to find your animal in the usual haunts. Just start walking around your neighbourhood and stop at any buildings, however unlikely. Your animal may be shut in where the pendulum gives a *'yes'* or *'this one'* response.

Wherever you get the *'yes'* response, call out to the animal. if you look daft so what? If there is no answer from the animal be especially alert for similar buildings especially if you get *'try-again'*.

I don't believe you need to invoke the powers of sympathetic magic by carrying a cat hair to find a cat, or indeed, a key to find a key. Some people have special pendulums with holes in for substances that are akin to those you are looking for. But the pendulum seems able to work out what you want without physical clues. After all it is fired by your inner abilities and if you are looking for your cat you are likely to be concentrating on that to the exclusion of everything else.

If the pendulum seems set on a particular spot check all round and if necessary ask at the house if there is a shed or other outbuilding. The cat may even be in the house having pretended to be abandoned if you've bought a cheaper brand of cat food than usual.

One of my cats, Hagel, is very unadventurous and not very bright. She rarely goes beyond the end of the road unless she is with the family (she accompanies us on walks and to the local shop). Since Hagel never misses mealtimes I knew she was lost quite early on.

I was drawn to a network of roads away from her usual haunts and as I walked I was attracted to a glass chalet at the bottom of a garden. So I called Hagel's name and I felt sure I heard her meow. But then there was silence so I went to the house. The owners insisted that the chalet was only open in the summer but I persisted and eventually they agreed to open up and there was Hagel under a workbench behind some planks. I never did discover how she managed to get there.

Day
38

Finding your way

As I have said, you could use your intuitions without the pendulum. But the pendulum does enable you to match your inner conviction with a physical response and since we are taught from an early age (perhaps wrongly) to trust only the evidence of our eyes, then the pendulum can give us the courage to trust our inner wisdom.

Your pendulum can help you to find your way or even choose one. While we may not have the amazing homing ability of the Alaskan salmon, who swims thousands of miles to return to her original river to reproduce, or the small birds who migrate across vast oceans. We women are remarkably good at instinctively detecting the right way. The old joke goes that you leave map-reading to the guys and then tell them where to go when they get lost. Of course many women are excellent map-readers just as some men use their instinctive inbuilt directional radar. But women do seem especially good at choosing the correct way when maps and signposts fail.

This ability tends to surface in times of crisis. Say, for example, mum is serving up Sunday dinner at one. Your new boyfriend's shortcut has left you with ten miles to go in ten minutes and you're stuck in a warren of country lanes that all end as No-Through roads.

Or it may be that the baby is yelling his head off and you've used the last disposable nappy twenty miles back. I'm sure you can insert your own crisis.

I came across the case of Rita, an American woman who was hopelessly lost and very upset, while trying to find her new adoptive son's foster home in Baltimore. Then she calmed herself down and instinctively found her way in a very short time across two counties. In spite of massive roadwork detours which were not on the map.

So if you need to find your way (sometimes it doesn't matter or you don't really want to get where you're going) first calm down.

If you're in a car and it's somewhere safe, try getting out and walking away. Then ask your pendulum if it would please point out the right direction. If you've got a cynical travelling companion, it's a good time to use your pendulum pendant or small pocket pendulum and rely on vibratory movements.

If you're relying on intuition via your pendulum, don't be tempted to combine it with map-reading until you're sure of the general direction. You don't see seagulls stopping to consult the Ordnance Survey map.

Again, the best results are need-driven. I can't follow even a simple map. On one memorable occasion I directed us to what I thought was a motorway but it turned out to be a river. The boyfriend for whom I was navigating was not amused.

But when we got lost in a hire car in the back streets of Pittsburgh, I automatically navigated us back to the main road. The need was particularly pressing at that time because the residents looked decidedly unfriendly towards strangers.

The male concerned still wasn't impressed. But had I hang-glided naked from the top of the Empire State Building, this particular guy would have pointed out that I was three centimetres off target and that my lipstick was smudged.

For most of us the pendulum will remain a personal guide for divination. For discovering remedies for our physical and stress ailments, and for those urgent times when we need keys or shoes, or our passport to jet off to a remote South Sea Island for an all expenses paid trip (I'm still dreaming).

Your pendulum is your best friend. It will answer your questions truthfully and with that unconscious wisdom that can enable you to avoid future pitfalls and recognise the right physical and spiritual path from a web of options. It is a part of you, an outward expression of your inner intuitive abilities. For at the end of the day you are your own best friend and guide.

Keep faith with yourself and love yourself for what you are and not what you might have been, or what other people tell you that you should become.

Ignore what other people tell you that you should be able to do with your pendulum and resist the tests that they may set. For the pendulum is not a party trick or just a tool of the outer world.

You may well know the answers to your own questions before you ask them, but your pendulum can guide you to the real issues and the best answers. Its test of success is whether it can help you to live your life according to your own light.

For when your pendulum reflects the sun or moon or rainbow colours they reflect the magic that is within you and that is beyond measure.

There are dowsers who say that you can detect ghosts using a pendulum. The expert, TC Lethbridge, recommended lengths of string which, he said, tuned into the ghostly wavelengths.

In my book *Psychic Suburbia* (published by Foulsham) I recount the story of Ron whose house was haunted by the spirit of a young woman. Ron told me: 'I was sceptical at first when three very nice ladies came with pendulums.

Pendulums and ghosts

'They walked around the house and told me which parts the spirits liked. They went into my son's bedroom and gave my wife the pendulum and she found it moving in very strange ways. I used to see the spirit next to my nine year old son Ben's bed when he was asleep.'

However, I was rather sceptical myself about the connection between pendulums and ghosts until I went to stay with my friends John and Daphne in Scotland. John is an expert dowser of the kind I had been suspicious about.

But while staying with them I became totally hooked on a glorious mixture of psychic and physical dowsing, that probably breaks all the dowsing rules but proved pretty powerful stuff.

One afternoon we went to a castle that had been turned into a hotel, Culcreuth Castle in Stirlingshire, not far from Loch Lomond. We went first into the Dungeon Bar and as I stood

Pendulums and ghosts under an archway I felt in one corner a terrible fear and coldness and that I was being crushed.

John didn't have his pendulum and so he asked the girl at the bar for a piece of string from which he suspended a key. He held his makeshift pendulum under the doorway and it pulled towards the corner and made very peculiar turns in the spot I had stood.

As the hotel was virtually deserted, Daphne, who had been talking to the girl behind the bar, arranged for us to go on a tour. The Chinese bedroom was said to be haunted by a young man playing a lute.

But instead of hearing ghostly music, I became aware of an old woman with an oatmeal coloured head-dress and a dull reddish long coarse robe, standing under the arch where the pendulum had pulled towards the corner.

She was in a dull haze but started to follow us and seemed to be shooing us out as if she didn't want us there. I didn't like to say anything though I hadn't had anything stronger than Scotch Broth.

When we entered the Organ Room I felt as though a force was blocking me. Daphne told me that wasn't uncommon, but again the pendulum reacted as the old woman was standing pushing us on.

On the second landing I shivered as she

stopped behind me and John's pendulum was again moving irregularly — apparently he and Daphne often noted reactions to 'cold spots'.

At the entrance to the Chinese bedroom I did not see the young man ghost but felt coldness and sadness and fear. The old woman was muttering and trying to shoo us on. She finally left us outside the house and turned into an old barn-type building I afterwards realised wasn't there.

When we were in the car and driving away, I inquired if the ghost of the castle was definitely male and Daphne asked me why. I explained about the old woman and Daphne said that, while John and I had been under the archway with the makeshift pendulum, the girl behind the bar had explained she was glad to see us as she'd been feeling very nervous.

She had seen the head and shoulders of a woman in fawn and some of the other staff had seen a woman recently.

I realised that the pendulum was probably giving physical expression to the natural psychic ability we all have. Probably I'll never get such verification of pendulum power again but that doesn't matter if our pendulum can help us to tune into other dimensions.

Should we be dabbling? It isn't scary and it isn't occult. It's only our present Western civilisation that insists on rigid demarcations

Pendulums and ghosts of dead and living and assumes the gates of heaven are one way only. You won't attract spirits only detect presences that are already there and many people believe what we are picking up is imprints of the people and scenes.

Not having the experience or confidence of Daphne and John I tried pendulum ghost 'tuning' — hunting is quite the wrong concept — at Hampton Court where I was involved in a broadcast from the Haunted Gallery. We drove in to the imposing grounds and I felt like a star at last (until my middle son threw up at the gates over my interview suit just as the outside broadcast vans came by).

But I was able to be alone for a while in the Gallery while the others were filming elsewhere and I got out my pendulum. Quite naturally I seemed to be drawn on a path that left me feeling agitated and very frightened outside some closed doors. I wanted to run and shout and bang on the door but resisted as it might not have created a positive impression on my first outside broadcast.

I knew that Catherine Howard, the young fifth Queen of Henry VIII, was said to haunt the Gallery and I wasn't surprised to discover from the curator that I had walked the path that the child bride had run in anguish after her arrest to hammer desperately on the Chapel Doors, begging for Henry to save her.

The King either didn't hear or ignored her, for

she was executed. But her sense of injustice and bewilderment were quite overpowering.

Your pendulum can tune you into the feelings of a place, like putting a coin in one of those audio-visual machines that recreate history.

A sudden drop in temperature in a certain spot may indicate that some presence or past memory is locked into that place. Start by going to your local haunted Castle or stately home. Of course, the ghostly presences will have been hyped up to attract visitors, but there's usually something that sparked the rumour in the first place.

Tuning in to presences

Like me at Culcreuth Castle, you may not pick up the star ghost but a servant. My old lady in fawn is just one of the hundreds of presences who probably inhabit any large house or castle, servants who grew up there and died in service and knew no other home.

Why shouldn't they return as well as the noble lords and ladies? After all, death is supposed to wipe out all social distinctions.

If you make a few discreet inquiries from the custodians or the lady in the tea-shop, you may find that others have seen your ghost.

You may feel in tune with a particular ghost, perhaps a the phantom of a mother if you are a mother yourself. Hold your pendulum wher-

Tuning in to presences ever you feel a cold place or simply follow a path and see where your pendulum leads. It will swing in the direction you should follow and perhaps make unusual movements at certain spots.

You probably won't see full-blown manifestations, certainly not if you don't want to. You may see a picture in your mind's eye or a flash of colour even hear an old song.

Unlike tuning into past lives, these glimpses of another era won't be connected with you, except that you may feel sympathy with certain characters and so perhaps share their feelings. The feelings won't always be sad. You may sense happiness, security in a much-loved nursery and even the laughter of children.

Once you are confident, you can move away from accredited ghost spots and pick them up all over the place. Why use a pendulum? Because it gives outward expression to your inner psychic abilities and can help you to locate particular places, like under my archway in Culcreuth Castle.

It is also useful in tracking a path trodden in history. I've taken my pendulum down an old track from the town of Freshwater to the bay and seen the old fisherwomen with their baskets. They didn't bother me nor were they even aware of me. A well-trodden trail has very strong imprints and as you walk with these old characters your own life is made richer. There is a sense that you are not alone here in the present, but part of a rich tapestry of kings nobles, servants and the vast majority of ordinary folk who have lived and loved.

Why go on a simulated journey through history when you can create your own?

Day 41

Pendulum psychometry

While I was in Scotland I also experienced pendulum psychometry. John had a wonderful collection of stones and rocks he'd gathered from all over Scotland. He gave me one piece and suggested I passed the pendulum round it. As I did so I felt very uncomfortable. It was like being enclosed and crushed. John said it came from a mine that had collapsed.

I was surprised by the reaction that I felt from John's mine rock. Many people find the idea of holding an object and sensing its past history alien and a bit artificial. I automatically block the instinctive psychometric powers we all possess because it is a big step in belief.

Passing a pendulum around or over an object focuses these natural abilities and can create in our mind's eye visual images. Or we may hear words in our mind that seem entirely unconnected but often hold the key.

Like all psychic abilities psychometry is spontaneous. To perform to impress friends or try to guess things about a pre-ordained object the person who gives it you knows about, is to

Pendulum psychometry create expectations of success that can block your instinctive knowledge.

When I picked up the information about John's stone, he was, in fact, asking me to pass the pendulum around the stone for a completely different purpose to do with its polarity. I have a knack of ruining experiments. For example, during an experiment with telepathy in which I took part for a radio station in the south west of England, GWR, 100 callers failed to guess the identity of a simple object which I had drawn. Dave Barrott, the radio presenter, swears that the object I'd drawn, a key, was totally unrecognisable to the eye, let alone telepathically.

But the experience with John gave me the confidence to use the pendulum as an aid to detective work in an old place. I found that it can be useful to pass a pendulum around a stone or even an ancient monument entirely without any pre-formed ideas. If you go with too definite a target in mind, psychometry can degenerate very rapidly into a game of psychic 20 questions.

Expert psychometrists do visit old sites and pick up impressions of its past. These may sometimes be confirmed archaeologically but what is important is to tune into an earlier way of life and share its feelings, rather than facts that no one can verify with 100 per cent certainty.

On a more personal level, you may find by passing your pendulum over gran's watch you feel close to her, or recall the colour of her cardigan or hear a favourite phrase of hers. You may even smell her perfume.

Contrary to popular practice, I think we all gain more from our own efforts than visiting an expert psychometrist, who may come up with some pretty amazing facts, but can't transmit the love coming down through a precious family treasure.

You will find the pendulum falls into a natural rhythm as you pass it round or hold it over an object. The pendulum may swing in a positive way or it may be quite still: we are not seeking *'yes'/'no'* responses but homing into something less tangible but very special. You will recognise it when you experience it.

Using psychometry to tune into the future rather than the past has not been fully explored. You might like to hold your pendulum over an object representing some desire, a baby shoe if you plan a child, a toy plane if you want to travel, a book if you are thinking of studying.

But the pendulum won't give you all the answers or imprint the book on your mind nor foretell if you will have a child.

What it can do, whether it makes a *'yes'* response or simply feels right, is to galvanise your inner energies to obtain the dream in real life. Your pendulum may vibrate strongly filling you with energy and determination.

However, if the pendulum seems to be giving a negative reaction — whether it's making a *'no'* response or simply feels wrong, then your inner wisdom is warning you that the time isn't right or perhaps at heart you want something different.

Try again in a few weeks or months. But if your pendulum still feels wrong, sit back and consider your goals and ambitions again. It's easy to confuse what we really want or need with the expectations of society and the wishes of those closest to us.

Day
42

Pendulums and ley lines

Before going to Scotland, I had understood leys, lines of energy running across the land on a theoretical level, but not felt them. Even circle dancing in Berkshire in a village hall where two leys were supposed to cross failed to raise so much as a psychic vibe.

John showed me how many hills had rocks on top and seemed to serve as markers for these older ways. I found myself being drawn along a particular path out in the wilds and it was heading between two distinctive markers. The pendulum marked out these energy lines and I felt very sad that I did not have the time to follow it.

So I decided when I got back to the Isle of

Wight to walk along the top of the Downs that bisect the Island and where there are many ancient burial mounds. I used a pendulum and found that I was being drawn to the different sites that were aligned though I'd never noticed and, as John had said, they were at regular intervals.

Along the paths I saw glimpses of ancient travellers. The pendulum rooted me in reality but seemed to guide my path as it took on a rhythmic swing. I followed a conventional route to the Mottistone, the ancient meeting place of the chieftains, but the pendulum didn't like it. Unlike me it wasn't deterred by brambles.

At the Mottistone I felt a dreadful sense of foreboding and the pendulum moved around alarmingly. Though the children were with me I didn't stay. Perhaps constant visitors had eroded its natural magic, perhaps darker things went on there that had left a mark, or perhaps the ancient chiefs didn't want me too near. It was time to back off and so I did.

And if you do feel a place is dark or unwelcoming be glad your pendulum has warned you. It won't attract harmful vibrations to you, but like any earthly place where we aren't welcome, it's a good idea to go where things feel happier.

From studying a map of your own area, you may find that churches and ancient monu-

Pendulums and ley lines ments are in a straight line. Whether you are an expert map reader or not, there's no substitute for going to the places and meeting the ley walkers of old for yourselves.

The path may not always be clear but the pendulum can usually guide you along the 'right road'.

And for me the important part about walking the leys, or whatever energy lines I'm following with my pendulum, is gaining a confidence that on a less tangible level I can find the right way.

If you go against a natural energy flow then any course will be more difficult. Walking the old paths is very positive if you've got decisions to make. Stop at each marker point and ask your pendulum a question about your own path whether at work or in a relationship.

It's harder to trace the old ways in a built-up area but you might find that churches and other prominent buildings are aligned. Any street map can help you to trace out a path but you will know it instinctively.

Alternatively, just as map dowsing works, you can draw circles on paper and use each one to represent an energy point. Write in each one a question or logical step and hold your pendulum over it. Your pendulum will use these inner leys to guide you to the right way.

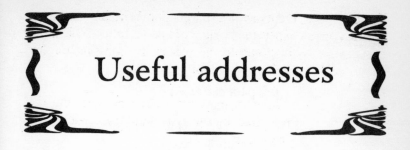

Useful addresses

As I said earlier, some people do believe that physical dowsing skills can be refined and that specific techniques can enable you to dowse for anything at any time. I believe you can gain the confidence to dowse successfully without a crisis to take your mind off the doubts. If you feel you want to explore this avenue you'd do well to contact one of the following dowsing associations:

The British Society of Dowsers
  Sycamore Cottage,
  Tamley Lane,
  Hastingleigh,
  Ashford,
  Kent. TN25. 5HW.
  Tel: 0233-75253.

The American Society of Dowsers
  Dowsers Hall, Danville,
  Vermont, 05828-0024.
  Tel: 802-684-3417.

I also mentioned that you might want to use alternative medicine in conjunction with the well-being aspects of your dowsing.

**Useful
addresses**

For information about complementary medicine, you could contact:

The Institute of Complementary Medicine,
   Telephone: 071-237-5165.

The National Association of Medical Herbalists
   34 Cambridge Road,
   London SW7.
   Tel: 071-228-4417.

The Homeopathic Development Foundation,
   19a Cavendish Square,
   London W1N 1RJ.
   Tel: 071-935-2163.

Finally, if you do want to go beyond the scope of healing in your personal sphere, I would suggest that you contact:

The British Alliance of Healing Associations,
   3 Sandy Lane,
   Gisleham,
   Lowestoft,
   Suffolk, NR33 8EQ.
   Tel: 01502-742224.

or

The National Federation of Spiritual Healers,
   Old Manor Farm Studio,
   Church Street,
   Sunbury on Thames,
   Middlesex TW16 6RG.
   Tel: 0932-783164.

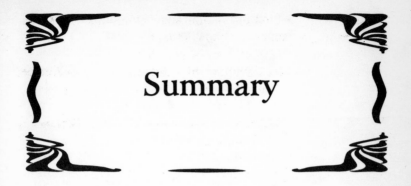

Summary

A pendulum can be any weight on a chain or cord. Possible pendulums include:

1. An old key or heavy curtain ring tied to a pencil with a length of cotton wound round it, secured with a paper clip.

2. A plumb bob on a piece of picture cord from the local DIY shop.

3. The most commonly-used pendulums are pointed-ended crystal ones, either lead or quartz crystal on a single ring and chain. You might prefer a crystal on a chain that you can always wear.

4. You can use any charm or medallion that has personal significance for a very personalised pendulum.

The Yes/No Response:

Let the pendulum swing in it's own time or give it an initial push. Eventually the pendulum may circle clockwise or anti-clockwise and which seems right (or occurs first) is the *'yes'* response. The opposite is often the negative response. Or for some people the pendulum makes ellipses or a mixture of both ellipse and circle. Listen to your inner-voice and it will tell you which is yes and which is no.

The Try-Again Response.

Sometimes we are asking the wrong question because the real issue is hidden or too painful to look at. If the question is masking a deeper issue, the pendulum will simply say *'try-again'* or 'What's the real question?' If your *'yes'*/ *'no'* is a circular movement, the try-again may be a wild ellipse. Or it may stop and vibrate mid-swing or even shoot off at a tangent. If you ask the pendulum it will show you. Or you may discover this third alternative the first time you ask a real question.

Using Your 'Yes'/'No' Response to Plan Your Future Path Using A Chart.

If an issue looks like being very complex develop a simple flow chart (following the track down *'yes'*/*'no'*/*'try-again'* to work through the options on offer. You can add an appropriate question at each crossroads. Don't try to plan the chart in advance or you will limit your intuitive thoughts.

Don't think too hard about the initial question. Write down whatever comes into your head. If a *'yes'*/*'no'*/*'try-again'* issue seems like becoming tangled you can start a flow chart at any stage in the proceedings.

Have a *'yes'* side and a *'no'* side of the paper.
Put *'try again'* directly under underneath the
main question as this is an intermediate stage
and go on to question 2. According to the
answer write down your next question again in
the *'yes'* or *'no'* column.

Deciding between more than two options:
Ask your pendulum to establish a *'this one'*
response to discriminate between options. Or
you can use the yes reply of the pendulum.

Making an Options Cloth
Use an old scarf or piece of cloth a foot to
eighteen inches square on which to draw your
three circles.

The Circle of Self
This represents the *inner world of the essential, real you,* that was you when you were five
and will be there when you are ninety five. If
your pendulum homes in here you'll know that
the way forward is by establishing your priorities and going it alone.

Circle of Interaction
This is where you *meet the outside world half-
way, the circle of negotiation and compromise.*
Sometimes it's hard to listen to what the other
person is really saying and not what you imagine they will say. This may also tell that your
ambitions and dreams have to take account of
the needs of those around you, whether it's a
temporary situation or a series of on-going
commitments.

Summary

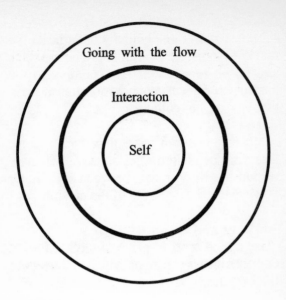

The Circle of Going with the Flow

This talks of *living for now on other people's terms and not standing out for your rights or going it alone*. There are times when it's best to go along with the way life is and not as we would like it to be. We can all waste time and energy on regrets and maybe if you look on the bright side you'll find it's better than you think.

The Outer Areas

These lie beyond the circles and can be used after a circle reading to identify the most appropriate course of action. You'll simply divide this area into four using the quarter of an hour positions on a clock. Each segment represents a different element, *Earth, Air, Fire* or *Water*.

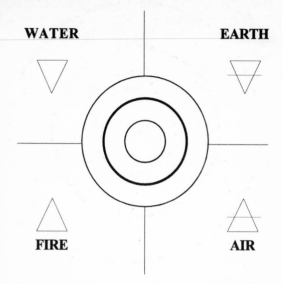

WATER　　　　**EARTH**

FIRE　　　　**AIR**

The Earth Quadrant

This represents the practical approach, whether drawing up rotas to make organisation of your daily work or home life more efficient and less of a burden for you, withdrawing practical help if you are doing more than your share, or if a cause is worthwhile, by rolling up your sleeves.

The Air Quadrant

This uses thought and logic rather than emotion. Once you have decided on action, *Air* insists that you go straight for it so your plans don't end up as a load of empty angry words or hot air. It's a signal to move back from an issue or decision especially if it involves a lot of emotion and weigh up the pros and cons as though you were advising someone else.

The Fire Quadrant

This tells you to use the solution that comes unbidden into your head. It represents the sudden change, the snap decision or simply the resolve not to be pressurised into answering right now if none the options feel right.

Rearrange the pieces, look at the issue from a new angle and try a third solution. Usually this will be one that you have already rejected as impractical or risky, but ultimately it may prove the best.

The Water Quadrant

This tells you that all may not be as it seems so dig below the surface so try to understand the underlying motives, fears and feelings of others.

Above all listen to your own gut feelings and intuitions as to whether a person or situation is to be trusted.

Let yourself go with the flow for now and see what happens.

Options Charts

If you want to focus on a specific issue or area of concern then you may want to make a quick personalised pendulum chart. You can make as many subdivision options as you wish and use the quadrants round the circles as well. Either like the ones on the pendulum cloth for *Earth, Air, Fire* and *Water*, or as extra option areas.

The Well-Being Cloth

The Inner Circle of *physical well-being*. The pendulum will respond here if the root of the problem is a physical one, for sometimes what we blame on stress can have a simple and often curable physical component.

The middle circle is *the area of mental well-being*. If the pendulum responds here, the root of your problem is stress. For worry, repressed anger or anxiety can lead to insomnia, over-eating or drinking or lack of appetite, a constant racing heart and pulse and muscle pain from being constantly poised for flight or fight.

You may find that the pendulum is drawn to both circles as physical ills can result from a combination of organic and environmental sources in which case you need to look to both areas.

Finding the Remedy.

Divide the outer circle into four, with lines at the 12, 3, 6 and 9 o'clock positions.

The 12-3 o'clock quadrant represents letting nature take its course. You can help matters along by getting plenty of rest, eating a sensible diet and avoiding unnecessary stress.

The 3-6 o'clock quadrant is the seek expert advice area either from your GP or alternative practitioner, maybe both.

Summary

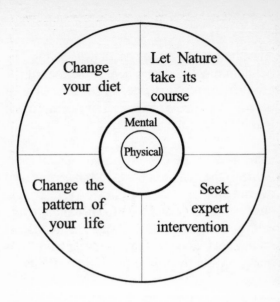

The 6-9 o'clock quadrant is the area of *Environmental Change*. If it's a stress problem then maybe you need to sort out the issue that's keeping you awake. Or if you cannot change the root of the problem, then perhaps you could practise relaxation or try to develop other more positive areas in your life to compensate.

The 9-12 o'clock quadrant concentrates on *Dietary* Issues since this is a prime candidate for all kinds of dis-ease both mental and physical in our lives.

In the quadrants of the outer circle, your pendulum may be drawn to more than one area if there are a combination of factors implicated. Try changes in the relevant practical sphere and see what improvements take place.

Today's Woman Divination series

Each is written in the same easy-to-follow style and, in a six-week course, concentrates on developing your powers of intuition rather than relying on expensive clairvoyants to choose your path for you.

Once you have learned one system, it is very easy to move on to the other forms of divination described in these books.

Rune Divination for Today's Woman

Many women don't use runes because they seem complicated. But by drawing simple symbols on pebbles you can tap into a magic that is as fresh today as when Anglo-Saxon women first tried to juggle relationships and family with the need for finding their own identity.

Tarot
Divination
for Today's
Woman

The ancient symbols of the Tarot can be adapted to the lives of women today, using a very simple spread to build up a picture of options available. For this is fortune-making, not fortune-telling and relies, not on some external magic, but on your own very powerful intuitions.

Crystal Divination for Today's Woman

Crystals and semi-precious stones provide a very powerful form of divination by harnessing the energies of your own powerful inner magic. You don't need to be an expert geologist to use the system which is based on a very simple colour method which you can adapt to your own special needs.

I Ching Divination for Today's Woman

Take away the image of the male Chinese civil servant which until now has dominated the I Ching and it reflects a woman's natural approach to magic and change. Using the more ancient system, based on the natural forces of fire, sky, water, earth, trees, thunder, mountains and lakes, women can interpret their own present and plan the future.

The book shows how to make simple I Ching pebbles to work out your trigrams in seconds.

Moon Divination for Today's Woman

Moon Divination puts women in touch with their natural inner cycles that, from the beginning of time, have been linked with the phases of the Moon. It uses Planet Stones made from ordinary materials and a Moon Cloth to harness the power of our inner astrology. But the book is not about worshipping a Moon Goddess. It deals with the everyday problems of modern women.

About the Author

Cassandra Eason is a mother of five children and lives on the Isle of Wight. She juggles writing and broadcasting with taking care of the family, and the vacuum cleaner with the word processor, and frequently ends up fusing both. From an ordinary home in the back streets of Birmingham, she won a scholarship to an exclusive school (her Dad's bike would be parked alongside the Rolls-Royces at Open Evenings).

She became a teacher and then married a nice middle-class boy but found out that nice china at tea-time wasn't the same as a warm heart. Cassandra was rescued from a tumbledown cottage in Cornwall with two small children by a middle-aged knight in a Renault 4 whom she later married. Together they had three more children.

While the children were small, Cassandra trained in psychology with the idea of returning to teaching. But she was pushed into a writing career when her middle son, Jack, told her that his dad was falling off his motor bike as it was happening 40 miles away.

The response to this experience from ordinary mothers led to her first book, *The Psychic Power of Children* which looks at the extraordinary psychic experiences of ordinary people. This book has now been re-published, in a revised version with many new cases, by Foulsham, along with its companion volume, *Psychic Suburbia*.

Her interest in divination methods grew while she was researching these books. Since the publication of the *Today's Woman* series, she has appeared on radio and television demonstrating her methods.